KT-379-936

UK PRICE
£3.99

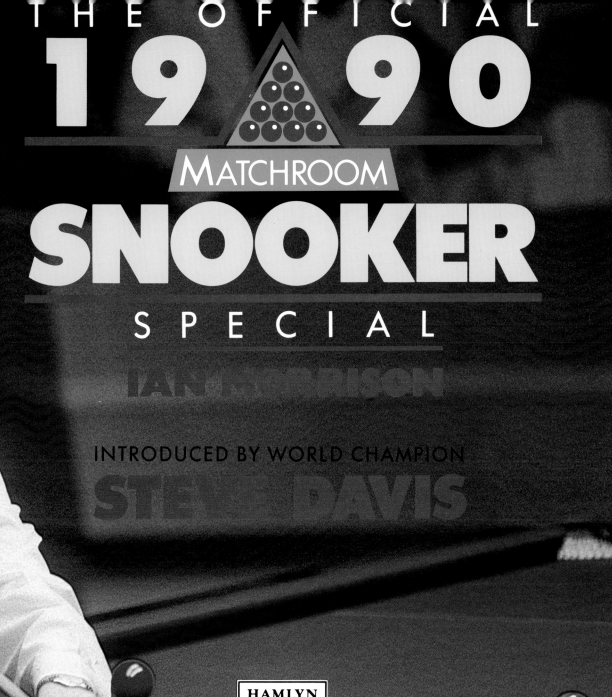

THE OFFICIAL 1990

MATCHROOM

SNOOKER

SPECIAL

IAN MORRISON

INTRODUCED BY WORLD CHAMPION

STEVE DAVIS

HAMLYN

Contents

Photographic acknowledgements

Front and back cover: Matchroom/Bob Thomas
Front cover inset: David Muscroft

Barry Hearn/Matchroom 55 top right; David
Muscroft Productions (incorporating the photo-
graphs of Trevor and Kevin Smith) Endpapers,
title page, 6-7, 8, 9, 11 bottom, 15 right, 16
bottom, 22, 23, 24, 25, 31, 32 right, 33, 34, 35,
36 top left, 38 top right, 38 bottom right, 40 left,
41 left, 42 left, 43, 44, 45, 46 left, 47, 49, 50, 51,
52, 53 top, 54, 55 bottom right, 56 bottom, 57,
58 left, 59, 60, 61 bottom; Terry Smith/TelSport
10, 14, 16 top, 17 left, 28, 29, 56 top; Eric
Whitehead 11 top, 12, 13, 15 left, 17 right,
18, 19, 20, 26, 27, 30, 32 left, 36 top right,
36-7 bottom, 38 left, 39, 40 right, 41 right,
42 right, 46 right, 48, 53 bottom, 54-5, 58 right,
61 top

Above **Matchroom in the frame. Relaxing are (from left) Willie Thorne, Jimmy White, Dennis Taylor, Neal Foulds, Terry Griffiths, Tony Meo and Steve Davis. This Magnificent Seven became the even more Magnificent Eight when Cliff Thorburn joined the team.**

Endpapers **The Crucible Theatre, Sheffield, home of the Embassy World Professional Championship. The audience awaits the players and referee.**

Title page **Steve Davis in the 1989 Embassy final. Steve won for the third successive year to register a record six championships at The Crucible.**

First published in 1989 by
The Hamlyn Publishing Group Limited
a division of
The Octopus Publishing Group Limited
Michelin House
81 Fulham Road
London SW3 6RB
and distributed for them by
Octopus Distribution Services Limited
Rushden
Northamptonshire NN10 9RZ

ISBN 0 600 56600 5   Printed in Great Britain

Foreword by
*Steve
Davis*

Barry decided the Matchroom players should draw straws to see who would write the foreword to this first *Matchroom Special*. I drew a long straw, but somehow, and I still don't know how, Barry worked out the job was down to me. He's like that. So feeling much like I do when I pot a long red only to go in-off into a baulk pocket, I had better start.

Actually, I'm delighted to be able to contribute a little to an annual which promotes the best snooker team in the world. And by 'team' I don't mean only the eight players at the sharp end, doing the business on the table. The players are in the spotlight and get plenty of publicity, anyway. But at Matchroom there is a very strong backroom team of chaps and girls who make the whole thing tick. Barry is at the helm, naturally. In case you didn't know, that's Barry Hearn, or as he's called around here, Barry 'Earn. Barry is quite well enough known himself, of course (you can't keep him off the telly!), but it's good to see some of the back-up team getting a little public attention. They deserve it.

Of course the *Matchroom Special* is also designed to help you get to know the players better – and I hope it gives you an idea of what we're like off the table, as well as on. On the playing side we picked up most of the major tournaments of the 1988-89 season, as usual. I was delighted to see Tony win his first major tournament, and was well pleased with my own form at the end of the season – not just because of the hat-trick of World titles, but because I think I played as well in the semi-final and final as at any time in my life. But it's not easy, I can tell you, even for the Matchroom team to keep winning and every year there are not only new players coming through to challenge us but sometimes 'old' ones getting a new lease of life. I'm thinking of Doug Mountjoy, of course. He had an excellent season, as this *Special* will show you. Because it's not only about the Matchroom boys. There's coverage of all the tournaments of the season – and if there were some we didn't win, well we've got to give credit where it's due.

By the same token you'll find not only profiles of the eight Matchroom players, but six of our main rivals as well. I speak for all the team when I say I hope you enjoy this *Matchroom Special*, and that knowing a bit about us all will add to your pleasure when you are watching us in the big events of the new season.

Steve Davis

MATCHROOM

STEVE'S THREE TONS

Trentham Gardens, Stoke-on-Trent, was the first stopping-off point on the 1988-89 ranking tournament tour.

Steve Davis was going for a second successive Fidelity win but had to come back from 3-1 down to beat his first opponent, Canadian Alain Robidoux, 5-4. "He's a player to watch for the future," said Steve.

Tony Meo came out of the wilderness with three good wins, but the "Whirlwind", Jimmy White, was upstaged by Malta's Tony Drago, who won a frame against Danny Fowler in just three minutes to set a new world record. Nevertheless Jimmy went on to meet Steve in a repeat of the 1988 final.

ALL-MATCHROOM FINAL

The all-Matchroom final saw Steve produce some of his finest snooker for a long time and he knocked in four centuries: 121, 108, 101, and 104. The last three came in consecutive frames, the first time Steve had achieved this in his illustrious career. They helped Steve run out the comfortable 12-6 winner to start the new season with the 18th ranking tournament success of his career.

HOW THEY FINISHED

Round 5

Steve Davis 5-1 David Taylor
Dennis Taylor 5-2 Jim Wych
Tony Meo 5-4 Bob Chaperon
Steve James 5-2 Stephen Hendry
Dean Reynolds 5-2 John Spencer
Joe Johnson 5-2 Steve Newbury
Barry West 5-4 Rex Williams
Jimmy White 5-4 **Willie Thorne**
Other Matchroom players: Cliff Thorburn not eligible; Terry Griffiths lost 5-0 to Jim Wych in the third round; Neal Foulds lost 5-3 to Dean Reynolds in the fourth round.

Quarter-finals

Steve Davis 5-2 **Dennis Taylor**
Steve James 5-1 **Tony Meo**
Dean Reynolds 5-1 Joe Johnson
Jimmy White 5-2 Barry West

Semi-finals

Steve Davis 9-1 Steve James
Jimmy White 9-5 Dean Reynolds

FINAL

Steve Davis 12-6 **Jimmy White**

First Prize: £45,000
Highest Break: 136 Dean Reynolds (v Tony Jones, Round 3)

Steve with the Fidelity trophy *(left)*, **the first ranking victory of the season. Tony Drago** *(right)* **set a world record with a three-minute frame against Danny Fowler. Tony Meo** *(below)* **began his good season by reaching the quarter-final.**

Match *of the Tournament*

Jimmy White v Willie Thorne (Round 5)

The opening two frames went to Willie. Jimmy pulled one back with an 81 break (surprisingly, the highest of the match) but Willie increased his lead to 3-1 thanks to breaks of 57 and 65. It was then Jimmy's turn and he drew level at 3-all by winning on the black in the sixth frame.

Jimmy went in front for the first time at 4-3 but Willie levelled it with a break of 59. And so it was down to the ninth and final frame.

Jimmy looked like taking the decider after potting the blue but he missed the frame-ball pink. Willie potted it but could not get on position for the black. It was 48-47 and all down to the last ball. The first and only error on the safety play came from Willie and Jimmy potted the black in the middle pocket for the match and a quarter-final meeting with Barry West.

QUOTES...
FROM MATCHROOM PLAYERS

"I never want to win a tournament and not beat Davis" . . . Jimmy White before his final meeting with Steve.

"I love playing Steve, he seems to bring the best out of me" . . . Dennis Taylor shortly before his quarter-final clash with Steve, who won 5-2.

"I have never scored three centuries in a row in practice – let alone in a tournament. I was shaking like a leaf when I reached the 70s in the third one" . . . Steve after compiling three consecutive centuries in the final against Jimmy.

"There was a time when I thought I couldn't improve but I have" . . . Steve after his win in the final over Jimmy.

MATCHROOM

Danny Falls 'Fowl' of a Whirlwind

It was off to Reading and the Hexagon Theatre for the second ranking tournament of the season. Because of behind the scenes squabbling there were no press interviews from the Matchroom players at Reading. But Steve did plenty of talking on the table, as he beat three Welshmen and two Irishmen to win the title.

SHOCKS GALORE!

The tournament provided plenty of shocks. Alain Robidoux, the man Steve tipped as being 'one to watch' went all the way from the first qualifying round to a semi-final with Alex Higgins.

Other shocks saw Nigel Gilbert, ranked 56 in the world, beat Silvino Francisco, Eddie Charlton and Tony Knowles, while Stephen Hendry lost to the rejuvenated Doug Mountjoy and John Parrott lost to Ray Edmonds, who enjoyed the best snooker win of his long career.

And what about Danny Fowler? After being on the end of Tony Drago's world record three-minute frame at Stoke, he felt the full force of the Matchroom "Whirlwind" at Reading. Perhaps Jimmy wanted to prove something – he "Whitewashed" poor Danny 5-0 in just 53 minutes, the quickest ever ranking tournament victory.

Rothmans Grand Prix

A STEVE v ALEX REVIVAL

The Higgins versus Davis matches in the early 1980s were legendary, and the two men met in the final – Alex's first major final since 1984. Sadly the excitement was missing as Steve continued his domination over the Ulsterman, stamping his authority in the first frame with a 137 clearance and racing into a 3-0 lead. Alex came back at him but Steve ran out the 10-6 winner as he continued his winning ways, taking his season's earnings to £225,000. For his efforts, Alex picked up £39,000, the biggest cheque of his 17-year professional career.

It was like old times as Steve and Alex (left) **met in the Rothmans final. Nigel Gilbert** (below left) **and Alain Robidoux** (below) **each did far better than their rankings would have suggested.**

HOW THEY FINISHED

Round 5

Alain Robidoux 5-4 Doug Mountjoy
Nigel Gilbert 5-4 Tony Knowles
Rex Williams 5-3 Ray Edmonds
Alex Higgins 5-3 **Neal Foulds**
Jimmy White 5-2 Jack McLaughlin
Dennis Taylor 5-2 Mike Hallett
Terry Griffiths 5-2 Eugene Hughes
Steve Davis 5-1 Cliff Wilson

Other Matchroom players: Cliff Thorburn not eligible; Willie Thorne lost to Gary Wilkinson 2-5 in Round 3; Tony Meo lost 5-0 to Alain Robidoux in Round 4.

Quarter-finals

Alain Robidoux 5-4 Nigel Gilbert
Alex Higgins 5-4 Rex Williams
Dennis Taylor 5-2 **Jimmy White**
Steve Davis 5-3 **Terry Griffiths**

Semi-finals

Alex Higgins 9-7 Alain Robidoux
Steve Davis 9-1 **Dennis Taylor**

FINAL

Steve Davis 10-6 Alex Higgins

First prize: £65,000
Highest Break: 139 Dean Reynolds (v Tony Knowles, Round 4)

Match of the Tournament

Alex Higgins v
Alain Robidoux (Semi-final)

The presence of these men in the semi-final had upset the form book, but the outsider Robidoux certainly didn't look like upsetting any more odds when Alex raced into a 7-0 lead at the end of the first session, aided by a break of 47 on his first visit to the table, and breaks of 86 in the fourth and seventh frames.

In the evening session the first frame belonged to the Canadian, but Higgins made it 8-1 and victory was in the bag. But then Robidoux staged a remarkable recovery to win six frames in succession. At 8-7, with the next frame finely poised, the Canadian had a "kick" on an easy red, and Alex took advantage and finished the match off with a break of 55. What a story it would have been if the ex-lumberjack Robidoux had reached the final after coming through every round of the tournament, including all the qualifying rounds.

QUOTES...
FROM MATCHROOM PLAYERS

Sorry, but there were no quotes from the Matchroom team during the Rothmans. As a result of legal action brought against the sponsors Rothmans following their decision to quit their sponsorship of the Matchroom League, Barry Hearn refused permission for his boys to give interviews.
Welshman Cliff Wilson, however, is entitled to voice an opinion of Barry: *"I hope he doesn't go out of snooker because the only other job he would want is God's, and that will take a bit of getting . . ."*

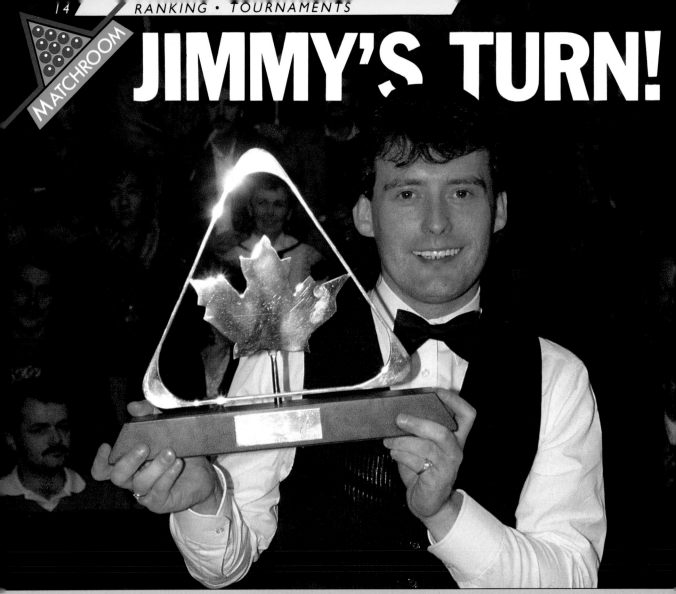

JIMMY'S TURN!

MATCHROOM

Canadian Master Jimmy White with his handsome trophy.

The Mikler Auditorium, Toronto, was the scene of the first ranking tournament ever to be staged outside Great Britain. And it was appropriate that it should be the scene of Cliff Thorburn's return to snooker after his two-match ban.

For economy reasons, only 32 qualifiers flew to Canada for the final stages. Some famous names were already out, but making the journey were a couple of surprise passengers: new professional Ian Graham, a former YTS shop assistant, and 59-year-old Liverpudlian George Scott, the man who helped develop John Parrott's game.

There was no fairytale ending for 'Scotty'. Steve Davis beat him 5-1. Graham, however, beat Eddie Charlton before pushing Cliff all the way to lose 5-4 after leading 3-0. Five of the eight quarter-finalists were Matchroom players.

CHAMPION v PRETENDER

One semi-final brought together Davis and the pretender to his throne, Stephen Hendry. Our Steve had to play some of his best snooker to prevent Hendry gaining win number two against him in 11 tries.

Steve looked likely to lose the 12th frame when trailing by 61 points and needing three snookers. Remarkably, he won it, making the score 7-5 instead of 6-all. From there he went on to win the match 9-5 and set up yet another Davis versus White final.

Jimmy had not beaten Steve since 1986, but he beat the world's number one by a convincing 9-4 margin, Steve's biggest defeat in a major final. For Steve, it ended a run of 22 matches without defeat in ranking events, and was his first defeat in a major final since he lost to Joe Johnson in the 1986 World final.

BCE Cananadian Masters

Match of the Tournament

Stephen Hendry v Cliff Thorburn (Quarter-final)

The biggest crowd of the tournament packed the Mikler auditorium in the hope of seeing their favourite Cliff reach the semi-finals.

Hendry won the opening frame, but Cliff led at 2-1, 3-2 and 4-3, when he had a great chance to win the match. He missed an easy black in its spot, and in stepped Hendry to level the match once more. The final frame was full of errors and excitement, the turning point coming when Cliff unluckily snookered himself with two reds left. Hendry cleared up with two visits to the table winning 61-51 on the final black. Both players received a standing ovation at the end of a tense match.

QUOTES...
FROM MATCHROOM PLAYERS

"I had some incredible flukes and I said sorry, something I don't normally do because I am a great believer in luck being shared out" . . . Steve after he beat Terry in the quarter-final.

After losing to Steve, Terry said: *"He's still the toughest man to play but after eight defeats in a row he's become a bit of a nuisance"*

"I am very nervous over nine frames and these short matches are brain damage to me" . . . Jimmy White after his close encounter with Dennis Taylor in quarter-final

"I owed him this one. I think I owed him about 20. This was a win I needed very badly" . . . Jimmy after his great win over Steve in the final

HOW THEY FINISHED

Round 5

Steve Davis 5-0 Steve James
Terry Griffiths 5-4 Doug Mountjoy
Cliff Thorburn 5-4 Ian Graham
Stephen Hendry 5-1 Cliff Wilson
Mike Hallett 5-2 Warren King
John Parrott 5-4 John Virgo
Dennis Taylor 5-2 David Taylor
Jimmy White 5-0 Steve Longworth

Other Matchroom players: Neal Foulds lost in Round 3 to Warren King 5-3; Tony Meo lost in Round 3 to Marcel Gauvreau 5-0; Willie Thorne lost in Round 4 to Doug Mountjoy 5-4.

Quarter-finals

Steve Davis 5-3 Terry Griffiths
Stephen Hendry 5-4 **Cliff Thorburn**
Mike Hallett 5-3 John Parrott
Jimmy White 5-3 **Dennis Taylor**

Semi-finals

Steve Davis 9-5 Stephen Hendry
Jimmy White 9-2 Mike Hallett

FINAL

Jimmy White 9-4 **Steve Davis**

First Prize: £40,000
Highest break: 132 Dennis Taylor (v David Taylor, Round 5)

Dennis lost to Jimmy in the quarter-final.   All his countrymen hoped Cliff would win.

MATCHROOM

MountJOY!

A happy Doug Mountjoy
with his Tennents trophy.
Doug's was the biggest
comeback for many a year.
Stephen Hendry *(below)*
played brilliantly to reach
the final.

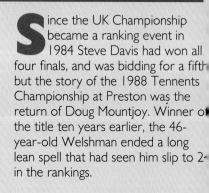

Since the UK Championship became a ranking event in 1984 Steve Davis had won all four finals, and was bidding for a fifth but the story of the 1988 Tennents Championship at Preston was the return of Doug Mountjoy. Winner of the title ten years earlier, the 46-year-old Welshman ended a long lean spell that had seen him slip to 2 in the rankings.

REVENGE FOR DOUG

Mountjoy started with a win over Neal Foulds, thus making amends for his 13-1 trouncing by Neal in the World Championship six months earlier. Mountjoy finished with a break of 121 and announced that his "best snooker days were to come".

Tennents UK Championship

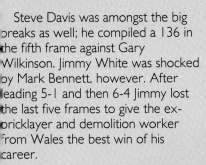

Steve Davis was amongst the big breaks as well; he compiled a 136 in the fifth frame against Gary Wilkinson. Jimmy White was shocked by Mark Bennett, however. After leading 5-1 and then 6-4 Jimmy lost the last five frames to give the ex-bricklayer and demolition worker from Wales the best win of his career.

THE MATCHROOM BOGEY MAN

Stephen Hendry set himself up as the bogey man of the Matchroom team by beating Thorne, Thorburn, and in the semi-final, Steve Davis, 9-3. To add to the gloom, Terry Griffiths went down 9-4 to Doug Mountjoy in the all-Welsh clash.

Mountjoy was appearing in his first final since the 1985 Benson and Hedges Masters. His re-found confidence stemmed from snooker *guru* Frank Callan, who brought him back from the edge of despair. He went on to outplay the young Scot in one of the game's most emotional wins. The £80,000 first prize was by far the biggest of his career; when he won the title in 1978 he collected £3,000.

Mark Bennett *(left)* **surprised Jimmy White in the fourth round. John Virgo** *(above)* **almost beat winner Mountjoy in the quarter-final.**

HOW THEY FINISHED

Round 5

Steve Davis 9-6 Danny Fowler
John Parrott 9-4 **Dennis Taylor**
Cliff Thorburn 9-8 David Roe
Stephen Hendry 9-4 **Willie Thorne**
Doug Mountjoy 9-5 Joe Johnson
John Virgo 9-3 Tony Knowles
Terry Griffiths 9-6 Dean Reynolds
Barry West 9-4 Mark Bennett

Other Matchroom players: Tony Meo lost 9-7 to David Roe in Round 3; Neal Foulds lost 9-4 to Doug Mountjoy in Round 4; Jimmy White lost 9-6 to Mark Bennett in Round 4.

Quarter-finals

Steve Davis 9-4 John Parrott
Stephen Hendry 9-2 **Cliff Thorburn**
Doug Mountjoy 9-8 John Virgo
Terry Griffiths 9-5 Barry West

Semi-finals

Stephen Hendry 9-3 **Steve Davis**
Doug Mountjoy 9-4 **Terry Griffiths**

FINAL

Doug Mountjoy 16-12 Stephen Hendry

First Prize: £80,000
Highest Break: 139 David Roe (v Matt Gibson, Round 2)

Match of the Tournament

Doug Mountjoy v Stephen Hendry (Final)

First blood went to the Welshman, who pulled away to 6-2 but then lost four in a row for 6-all. Hendry had been playing well all week and there were few who would have betted against the 4-1 on favourite. His 129 break levelled it at 7-all at the half-way stage.

The first session of the second day saw Mountjoy string together a great run of seven consecutive frames as he went to 14-7 and within two of the finishing post. His 131 in frame 20 was to earn the Welshman an extra £8,000 as the highest televised break.

The final session saw Mountjoy start with his third consecutive hundred (equalling Steve Davis' performance at Stoke), but with one frame needed Hendry came back at him again and won five frames on the trot to make it 15-12. The pressure showed in Doug's face, but in the next frame he got in with a break of 39 which soon took him to the title and a memorable win.

QUOTES...
FROM MATCHROOM PLAYERS

"He kept me off the table for long spells and that is what I normally do to other players. Occasionally I need performances like this against me. I need to fight against complacency." Steve after his semi-final defeat by Stephen Hendry.

After being pushed all the way by David Roe in the 5th round Cliff commented: *"Where are these young guys coming from. I can't remember the last time I played someone over 30!"*

"I don't think I've had a worse 18 months. If I can stay in the top 16 I'll be there for life." Comments from Neal after winning six frames in succession to beat the former English amateur champion Mark Rowing to reach the televised stage of the Tennents.

MATCHROOM

All but two of the Matchroom team reached the televised stage of the Mercantile Credit Classic at Blackpool's Norbreck Castle Hotel. And would you believe that the two were Steve and Jimmy . . . The result A second final without a Matchroom representative. And that man Doug Mountjoy crept in to win his second successive tournament.

HAPPY NEW YEAR

Steve crashed out of the tournament in the pre-televised stage to Welshman Tony Chappel 5-3 on New Year's Day. The Welshman was ranked 51 in the world at the time, but played some exhilarating snooker to beat the defending champion who was going for a hat-trick of Mercantile wins. Jimmy lost to Wayne Jones, who then went all the way to the final. The Welsh continued to be the scourge of the

Wayne reached his first ranking final to face old friend Mountjoy.

Willie Thorne was Wayne Jones's second Matchroom victim, losing in the semis.

FINAL SCORE:
Abertysswg 2
Rest of World 0

Mercantile Credit Classic

Matchroom men as Dennis lost on the final black to Steve Newbury, a semi-finalist 12 months earlier.

Ray Reardon put up a battle against Stephen Hendry before losing 5-4 but the Welsh had five men in the last 16. One who fell was Terry Griffiths who lost to stablemate Willie Thorne, who compiled a break of 134.

WELSH FAIRY TALE

Cliff and Willie both reached the semis to maintain the Matchroom record of having two semi-finalists in every ranking tournament this season. But that was as far as they went as Mountjoy and Jones progressed to the first all-Welsh final since 1980.

For both players it was like a dream. Jones had never been beyond the last eight of a ranking tournament before. As for Mountjoy – who would have imagined at the start of the season that he would appear in successive finals? Furthermore, he went on to win a second successive tournament, something only Steve Davis has done in the past.

"The Tennents was a fairy-tale", said Doug before the match. "You can't have two fairy-tales. Or can you?" . . . Oh yes, Doug, you can.

HOW THEY FINISHED

Round 5

Paddy Browne 5-1 Tony Chappel
Doug Mountjoy 5-4 Tony Knowles
Cliff Thorburn 5-3 John Virgo
Stephen Hendry 5-1 Steve Newbury
Martin Clark 5-3 Joe Johnson
Willie Thorne 5-1 **Terry Griffiths**
John Parrott 5-1 Silvino Francisco
Wayne Jones 5-3 David Taylor

Other Matchroom players: Steve Davis lost 5-3 to Tony Chappel in round 3; Jimmy White lost 5-3 to Wayne Jones in round 3; Dennis Taylor lost 5-4 to Steve Newbury in round 4; Neal Foulds lost 5-4 to Martin Clark in round 4; Tony Meo lost 5-1 to Silvino Francisco in round 4.

Quarter-finals

Doug Mountjoy 5-3 Paddy Browne
Cliff Thorburn 5-4 Stephen Hendry
Willie Thorne 5-4 Martin Clark
Wayne Jones 5-4 John Parrott

Semi-finals

Doug Mountjoy 9-5 **Cliff Thorburn**
Wayne Jones 9-4 **Willie Thorne**

FINAL

Doug Mountjoy 13-11 Wayne Jones

First prize: £55,000
Highest Break: 143 Nigel Gilbert (v Jack Fitzmaurice, Round 2)

Match of the Tournament

DOUG MOUNTJOY v WAYNE JONES (Final)

This was a match that captured the nation's hearts. The armchair fans were treated to a match that would make them happy no matter who won.

The appearance of Jones, ranked 34 in the world, gave hope to those on the way up, while the appearance of Mountjoy gave hope to those who might have thought they were on the way down!

The final was closely fought between two men who began their careers at the tiny Abertysswg Working Men's Club, and who used to spend five hours a day practising together.

When Jones pulled away at 11-9 it was the first time either player had opened a two-frame margin. But then the mental barrier perhaps blocked Wayne as Doug won the final four frames to take a memorable final between two popular Welshmen.

A happy Doug Mountjoy with his cheque and trophy after winning his second successive tournament.

QUOTES... FROM MATCHROOM PLAYERS

After losing to Tony Chappel in the pre-televised stage Steve Davis said of his conqueror: *"Tony was superb. I would have enjoyed watching him if it hadn't been against me"*

"There were times when I was losing that I thought 'Do I need this?' Then I think of the money; it's money for old rope. I can't believe how well we get paid for doing something we enjoy" . . . Neal Foulds

MATCHROOM

As Slick as a Parrott

Originally planned for Belgium, the European Open was eventually played at the Deauville Casino. Sadly, the French were not ready. Attendances for the first ranking tournament on the Continent were disappointing.

At the last minute ICI stepped in with some sponsorship, but only from the quarter-final stage onwards, when the event received television coverage.

Because of heavy commitments, Steve Davis gave the tournament a miss, and other notable absentees were John Spencer, Wayne Jones and Dean Reynolds.

The organisation left quite a bit to be desired, and Tony Meo, thinking he was a day early for his match with David Roe, was swept into the Casino immediately upon arriving, to find he had already forfeited two frames for a late arrival. Understandably, he crashed out of the event after only a couple of hours on French soil.

HOPPALONG HIGGINS

To make matters even more farcical Alex Higgins, who had recently broken a foot, made the trip to France and played hopping around the table on one leg. After beating the unfortunate Les Dodd, Higgins was eliminated by Willie Thorne, whose 5-0 defeat of Bill Oliver in the previous round was the second fastest (59 minutes) ever in a ranking tournament.

Dennis Taylor lost in the fourth round to the 'man of the season' Doug Mountjoy, but Cliff Thorburn ended the Welshmen's great run in the next round. Terry Griffiths had a great win over Martin Clark in the quarter-final, compiling two centuries in the first three frames.

John Parrott with his first major title, the ICI European Open. The new world number 2 enjoyed a good season.

EUROPEAN OPEN WINNER

ICI European Open

A GREAT ALL-MATCHROOM SEMI

n the semi-final Terry had a great
attle to beat Jimmy White. The
ther semi was also a nail-biting
ffair. John Parrott, twice beaten in
ajor finals this season, was
etermined to get his name on a
rophy and after coming back from
-0 and 4-3 down against team-mate
Mike Hallett he reached the final,
where he promised Terry a tough
match. And that's just what it was. . . .

Griffiths won the first three frames
nd led 4-1 before Parrott levelled at
-all. Terry then led 8-7 with two to
lay but the Liverpudlian showed
reat composure to clinch the last
wo frames and his first major title.

Match of the Tournament

Jimmy White v Terry Griffiths (Semi-final)

The final itself was certainly a
match to savour, but for a
match that had everything the White-
Griffiths semi-final was a must for all
nooker fans. Sadly, there weren't
oo many of them at the Deauville
Casino to see it.

Both men were playing with
confidence: Jimmy's 136 against Eddie
Sinclair in Round 3 was the highest
break at Deauville. Jimmy took the
irst frame with a 52. Terry levelled
with a 71 and then took the lead
thanks to a great 110.

But the next two frames belonged
to White, who took the lead at 3-2
with a break of 47 which was in
response to Griffiths' 52. Breaks of
58 and 39 gave Terry the lead back,
and a straight pink looked like the
end for White. But Terry missed and
Jimmy took the last two balls to level
at 4-all. And so to the decider.

Griffiths played some magnificent
safety play in the deciding frame and
t was White who made the first
error. Griffiths pounced to make a
break of 53 – good enough to take
the match.

HOW THEY FINISHED

Round 5
Eddie Charlton 5-4 John Virgo
John Parrott 5-0 John Campbell
Jim Wych 5-4 Danny Fowler
Mike Hallett 5-3 Stephen Hendry
Martin Clark 5-4 Joe Johnson
Terry Griffiths 5-3 Alain Robidoux
Cliff Thorburn 5-0 Doug Mountjoy
Jimmy White 5-3 Willie Thorne
Other Matchroom players: Steve Davis did not
compete; Tony Meo lost 5-1 to David Roe in
Round 3; Neal Foulds lost 5-3 to Martin Clark
in Round 3; Dennis Taylor lost 5-3 to Doug
Mountjoy in Round 4.

Quarter-finals
John Parrott 5-1 Eddie Charlton
Mike Hallett 5-3 Jim Wych
Jimmy White 5-3 **Cliff Thorburn**
Terry Griffiths 5-1 Martin Clark

Semi-finals
John Parrott 5-4 Mike Hallett
Terry Griffiths 5-4 **Jimmy White**

FINAL
John Parrott 9-8 **Terry Griffiths**

First Prize: £40,000
Highest Break: 147 Alain Robidoux (v Jim
Meadowcroft, Round 1)

QUOTES... FROM MATCHROOM PLAYERS

Terry on his recent run of success:
"Annette (his wife) *was sick and
tired of me losing and she told me
to put more work in. So I have put
in loads of practice."* He also added:
*"I've worked hard at my game
because as you get older, the game
becomes more difficult."*

Making reference to the sparse
crowds at Deauville, Cliff said after
his win over Murdo Mcleod: *"I was
watched by six people out there. My
gates are going up!"*

Of "Hoppalong Higgins", John Parrott
said: *"I wonder if Alex would mind if
I jumped on his shoulder?"*

Higgins *(above)*
**played on one leg
with a broken
foot until
eliminated by
Willie Thorne**
(right), **who won
his first match in
under an hour.**

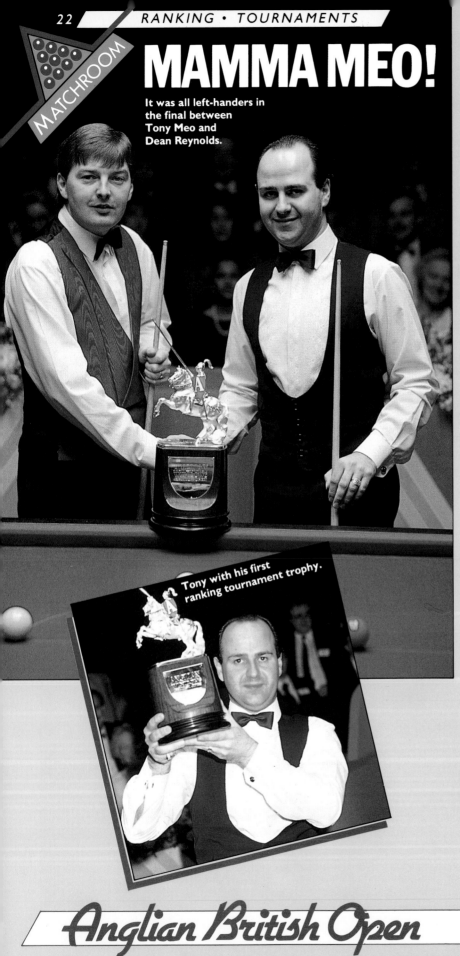

MATCHROOM

MAMMA MEO!

It was all left-handers in the final between Tony Meo and Dean Reynolds.

Tony with his first ranking tournament trophy.

With the track record of the Matchroom team it was a good bet that one of the boys would reach the final of the last ranking event before the world championship. But what odds would the bookies have given for him being Tony Meo, who will be the first to admit that the last two years have been a sheer nightmare for him? It was great to see him come from nowhere to win his first ranking tournament.

TONY FLIES THE FLAG

It was a good job Tony had such a good tournament because the rest of the team fell away before the semi-final stage. Dennis and Terry both went out at the first hurdle: Terry lost 5-1 to the ex-public schoolboy Mark Johnston-Allen, who went on to compile the tournament's highest break, 140, in his next match with Eugene Hughes.

A bout of food poisoning forced Jimmy White to scratch. Cliff lost 5-4 to Mike Hallett and Neal Foulds went down by the same score against Martin Clark.

Steve beat Willie 5-0 in Round 5 but the result of the round was Tony's magnificent 5-3 win over Stephen Hendry.

PARROTT BEATS DAVIS . . . AT LAST

Tony maintained the momentum in the quarter-final with a 5-3 win over the South African Peter Francisco, who was having an unlucky season, and was our only representative in the last four when Steve suffered his first defeat in six meetings against John Parrott, who inflicted a 5-1 defeat on him.

TWO CLASSIC SEMI-FINALS

Both semi-finals were classics, and both went the full 17 frames.

The final frame of the Parrott-Reynolds match lasted over 35 minutes before Reynolds got in to take the match 9-8.

Anglian British Open

In the other match, Tony looked to be out of it when trailing 6-8 and 1-58, needing a snooker to stay in the match. He got it, won the frame and went on to win the next two to register a great 9-8 win.

In the first ranking final between two left-handers, Tony built up a 10-4 lead at the end of the first day and soon finished off the Humbersider to defy his odds of 200-1 and become the 1989 British Open champion.

The final was marred by comments from Reynolds about him being bored during the match. But no attack on Tony could take the title away from him.

HOW THEY FINISHED

Round 5

Tony Meo 5-3 Stephen Hendry
Peter Francisco 5-1 Barry West
Mike Hallett 5-4 **Cliff Thorburn**
Martin Clark 5-4 **Neal Foulds**
Dean Reynolds 5-0 Cliff Wilson
Joe Johnson 5-2 Mark Johnston-Allen
John Parrott 5-2 Doug Mountjoy
Steve Davis 5-0 **Willie Thorne**
Other Matchroom players: Terry Griffiths lost 5-1 to Mark Johnston-Allen in Round 3; Dennis Taylor lost 5-4 to Colin Roscoe in Round 3; Jimmy White scratched after Round 3 (indisposed).

Quarter-finals

Tony Meo 5-3 Peter Francisco
Mike Hallett 5-3 Martin Clark
Dean Reynolds 5-4 Joe Johnson
John Parrott 5-1 **Steve Davis**

Semi-finals

Tony Meo 9-8 Mike Hallett
Dean Reynolds 9-8 John Parrott

FINAL

Tony Meo 13-6 Dean Reynolds

First Prize: £70,000
Highest Break: 140 Mark Johnston-Allen (v Eugene Hughes, Round 4)

John Parrott *(left)* **and Mike Hallett** *(below)* **each lost a semi-final 9-8 after leading 8-6.**

Dean Reynolds v John Parrott (Semi-final)

Either semi-final could have been "Match of the Tournament". In each the eventual winner came back from a 6-8 deficit to win 9-8. But the Reynolds-Parrott match has the edge because of the sheer brilliance of the tactical play of both players in the 17th and final frame.

Reynolds opened the match by taking the first frame 132-0. He led 3-1 before the Liverpudlian won four frames in succession to lead 5-3.

These two men know each other's game well, being pioneers of the Junior *Pot Black* programme in the early 1980s.

Parrott pulled away at 7-4, and went 8-6 up with three to play. Reynolds won the next two to make it 8-all – and so to that brilliant last frame.

The reds were scattered all around the table. Even the baulk area was no safe place to take the cue-ball and the most accurate of safety shots were needed. Both men played with skill, awaiting that fatal mistake from their opponent. Sadly for Parrott it was his error that finally let Reynolds in to clinch the match and deprive Parrott of a second successive ranking final. For Reynolds, it was his first ranking final and that meeting with Tony Meo.

QUOTES...
FROM MATCHROOM PLAYERS

In reply to the attack on him by Dean Reynolds after the final, Tony Meo said: *"My highest break was 84. But so what? I'm the British Open champion."*

Another quote from Tony after his great win: *"When I started this game I used to go for my shots all the time. It's all right being a crowd pleaser but if you don't win where does that get you?"*

MATCHROOM

Steve makes it six at The Crucible

Left **Steve with two treasures: girlfriend Judie Greig and the World Championship Cup.**
Above **Steve in the final against John Parrott.**

No man had won three consecutive world titles at The Crucible. That was one of Steve Davis' goals. Another was to win a sixth world title, which would equal Ray Reardon's modern-day record.

Steve had not won a tournament in 1989 and there were those pundits who were all too ready to write him off – as usual. But when it comes to the The Crucible there is only one master. It is like a second home to Steve and he proved once again why he is the best player in the world.

ANOTHER HENDRY-DAVIS CLASH

A potentially awkward opening match against Steve Newbury proved less of an obstacle than anticipated. Steve Duggan and Mike Hallett provided little opposition as Steve reached the semi-final and another meeting with Stephen Hendry. Hendry had started to get the better of Steve in recent meetings. But not this time. The world number one played some outstanding snooker to win 16-9.

The other semi-final saw John Parrott meet the revitalised Tony Meo. Sadly for Tony, after a great run, it was the Liverpudlian who went through to the final. Consolation for Tony was that his first World Championship semi-final appearance was enough to take him back into the top 16 in the rankings.

ALEX ABSENT

The 1989 Championship did not spring too many surprises. Perhaps the biggest was the absence of Alex Higgins at The Crucible at all. He had to pre-qualify for the first time and was eliminated by newcomer Darren Morgan, the day after Alex had won the Benson and Hedges Irish Masters.

PARROTT'S GOAL...

John Parrott started the 1989 Crucible campaign the day after the dreadful Hillsborough disaster in the same city. An ardent Liverpool follower he set out to win the world title in memory of those 95 Liverpool fans who lost their lives.

Understandably he was visibly affected by the disaster at first but as the tournament progressed he looked a potential Champion. But in the final he came up against a Steve Davis who produced wonder snooker.

The final was over in three sessions as Davis went from 5-2, to 13-3 and then to a Championship-winning 18-3. Parrott was unable to prevent Davis registering the biggest winning margin at The Crucible.

Tony Meo's successful season continued, as he reached the semi-final against John Parrott.

HOW THEY FINISHED

Round 1

Steve Davis 10-5 Steve Newbury
Jimmy White 10-5 Dene O'Kane
Steve Duggan 10-1 Cliff Wilson
John Virgo 10-4 Darren Morgan
Mike Hallett 10-7 Doug Mountjoy
David Roe 10-6 Tony Knowles
John Parrott 10-9 Steve James
Dennis Taylor 10-3 Eugene Hughes
Eddie Charlton 10-9 **Cliff Thorburn**
Terry Griffiths 10-6 Bob Chaperon
Tony Meo 10-5 Joe Johnson
Silvino Francisco 10-5 Joe O'Boye
Willie Thorne 10-5 Paddy Browne
Wayne Jones 10-9 **Neal Foulds**
Stephen Hendry 10-9 Gary Wilkinson
Dean Reynolds 10-7 Peter Francisco

Round 2

Steve Davis 13-3 Steve Duggan
Jimmy White 13-12 John Virgo
Mike Hallett 13-12 David Roe
John Parrott 13-10 **Dennis Taylor**
Terry Griffiths 13-9 Silvino Francisco
Tony Meo 13-8 Eddie Charlton
Dean Reynolds 13-3 Wayne Jones
Stephen Hendry 13-4 **Willie Thorne**

Quarter-finals

Steve Davis 13-3 Mike Hallet
Stephen Hendry 13-5 **Terry Griffiths**
John Parrott 13-7 **Jimmy White**
Tony Meo 13-9 Dean Reynolds

Semi-finals

Steve Davis 16-9 Stephen Hendry
John Parrott 16-7 **Tony Meo**

FINAL

Steve Davis 18-3 John Parrott

First Prize: £105,000
Highest Break: 143 Darren Morgan (v Alex Higgins, Qualifying Round 5)

QUOTES...
FROM MATCHROOM PLAYERS

After his marathon 10 hour first round match with Eddie Charlton, Cliff Thorburn said: *"When I started playing in the match I had a suntan. Now I don't have one."* When Charlton saw he was drawn against Cliff he said: *"I took odds the match would never end!"*

"My snooker a month ago was not good enough to win the world title. Now I have played the best snooker of my career." Steve Davis after winning the title for the sixth time.

Of Steve, Mike Hallett said after crashing out 13-3 in the quarter-final: *"I don't think he is playing as well as last year and he can be beaten."*

Match *of the Tournament*

Steve Davis v John Parrott (Embassy final)

When Steve beat Jimmy to win the first ranking tournament of the season, the Tennents, he described his play as 'the best of his career'. But in the final of the Embassy World Championship at The Crucible he produced snooker that only he could.

John Parrott was regarded as a serious challenger to Steve's world crown. But Davis destroyed the Liverpudlian with an 18-3 victory. The story of the final is simple. It was one-sided and the best man won – by miles!

Steve's potting was as sharp as ever and his safety play was impeccable. At the end of the first day the match was being declared a 'no contest' – and that is just what it was.

The score-line does John Parrott no justice. On the day the clinical approach of the ultimate professional was just too good for him and as Davis said: "I have reached a standard which I didn't think possible". No man could have offered a challenge to Davis the way he played, not even the number two in the world, John Parrott.

HOW THE REST OF

The 1988-89 season saw the introduction of some new non-ranking tournaments, like the Everest World Match-Play Championship, to go alongside some old favourites, like the Benson and Hedges Masters at Wembley.

The close-season saw John Parrott maintain his fine **Pontins** record by beating Mike Hallett 9-1 to win the professional title. He came close to the Open title as well, but lost to Colin Morton in the semi-final.

Other close-season tournaments saw Mike Hallett lose yet another final. This time he went down 6-1 to stablemate Stephen Hendry in the **New Zealand Masters** at Wellington. Still abroad, seven of the eight Matchroom men (Cliff was the odd one out) travelled to Hong Kong for the **LEP Hong Kong Masters**. With John Parrott, they competed in a 16-man tournament, the other eight being local players. Jimmy White collected the winner's £30,000 cheque following his 6-3 final win over Neal Foulds, who picked up £12,000.

NEW AUSTRALIAN AND CANADIAN CHAMPS

Australia and Canada had new champions. John Campbell regained the **Australian Professional Championship** with a 9-7 win over Robbie Foldvari in the final. And at the Mikler Auditorium, Toronto, Alain Robidoux beat Jim Wych 8-4 to win the **Canadian Professional Championship** at the first attempt.

At the Deauville Casino, Jimmy White was attempting to do what Steve Davis couldn't do the previous year, that is beat the American pool expert Steve Mizarek in the **Fiat Snooker/Pool Triathlon.** Mizarek won the straight- and eight-ball pool 2-0 and 3-0 respectively. Jimmy could have levelled with a 5-0 win at snooker, but Mizarek sneaked a frame to win the triathlon 6-4.

The governing body introduced two **WPBSA Non-ranking Tournaments** in 1988. There were no Matchroom players present at either event because of commitments elsewhere.

The first tournament, at Marco's Leisure Centre, Glasgow, attracted 47 entrants. Gary Wilkinson took the £5,000 first prize by beating Alex

The Wembley arena, snooker's biggest, used for the Benson and Hedges Masters. Jimmy's quarter-final battle with John Parrott was watched by 2,388 fans.

Higgins 5-4 on the final black. Alex was in another spot of bother for failing to give a urine sample for a drugs test.

Pontins, Brixham, was the setting for the second tournament. Higgins gained revenge over Wilkinson by beating him in the last 16 but then fell at the semi-final stage to Peter Francisco who, in turn, lost to the revitalised and 're-shaped' Irishman Paddy Browne by five frames to one in the final.

THE SEASON WENT

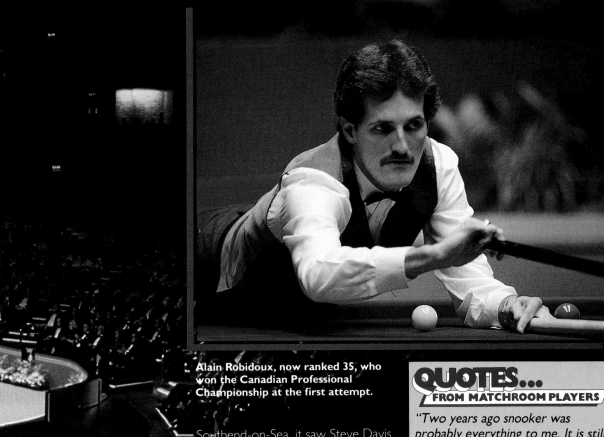

Alain Robidoux, now ranked 35, who won the Canadian Professional Championship at the first attempt.

MIKE WINS AT LAST

Mike Hallett eventually won a tournament when he beat John Parrott and Stephen Hendry to land the £12,500 first prize in the **Fosters Professional Championship.** A four-man event, this was an old tournament with a new name. It was formerly the Carlsberg Challenge, and then the Carling Challenge.

Our own in-house **Matchroom Championship** was sponsored for the first time by LEP, who contributed £130,000 in prize money.

Played at the Cliff's Pavilion,

Southend-on-Sea, it saw Steve Davis compile a break of 132 in his opening game against Willie Thorne and serve notice of his intention to win one of the few titles to have eluded him. Steve went all the way and beat defending champion Dennis Taylor 10-7 in the final. Along with the trophy, Steve collected a cheque for £50,000.

After this it was off to Dubai for the eight Matchroom men to take part in the **Dubai Duty Free Masters.** Eight local players made up the entrants to 16.

Despite their keenness, the locals failed to take a frame off their more illustrious opponents. The tournament belonged to Neal Foulds, who played some of his best snooker for a long time and beat Cliff Thorburn and Tony Meo before enjoying a great 5-4 win over Steve Davis to take the £25,000 winner's cheque. ▶

MATCHROO

THE BIG MONEY

Undoubtedly the biggest non-ranking tournament of the season was the **Everest World Match Play Championship** at Brentwood, Essex.

The event came in for criticism because it incorporated the word "World" in its title, yet was open only to 12 players. Those 12, however, were the top 12 based on 1987-88 performances. The quality field was playing for a first prize of £100,000, the biggest winner's cheque in snooker history.

Six of the entrants were from the Matchroom stable, with only Neal and Tony missing. Mike Hallett knocked out Willie in the first round and before his clash with Steve in the next said: "I've watched Davis on video and I think I might have found the secret to beat him." Mike must have been watching the wrong video . . . Steve won 9-2 to add to recent 9-3, 9-0 and 13-1 wins over the Humbersider.

In another quarter-final, Jimmy beat Terry in an all-Matchroom affair. It was revenge for Jimmy after the semi-final of the World Championship earlier in the year, a defeat which Jimmy said "stung for three months".

In the semi-finals Steve avenged his Canadian Masters final defeat with a 9-5 win over Jimmy while John Parrott reached his second major final with a 9-6 win over Stephen Hendry.

Parrott trailed 0-6 in the final but staged a mini-revival before Steve ran out the 9-5 winner. It was Steve's fourth win of the season and the £100,000 cheque boosted his winnings to £373,000. For Parrott he had the consolation of the biggest cheque of *his* career, £40,000, plus another £10,000 for the highest break (135 compiled in the final).

Snooker welcomed back Norwich Union in 1988 as sponsors of the inaugural **Norwich Union European Grand Prix.**

A Matchroom-only event, four players at a time played qualifying matches at European venues. Dennis

Two shots of Jimmy with the American pool player Steve Mizarek. Jimmy and Steve played each other at snooker and pool at the Deauville Casino for the Fiat Snooker/Pool Triathlon. Steve won and has the Cup (above). 'Off-duty' the two enjoyed some fishing (right).

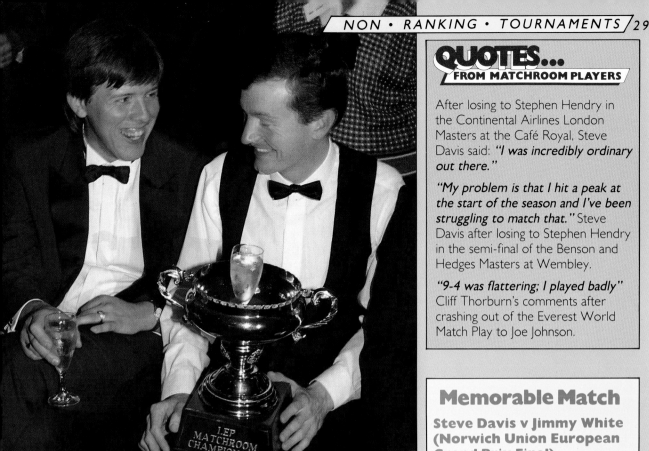

Steve relaxing with Neal after winning the Matchroom Championship.

QUOTES...
FROM MATCHROOM PLAYERS

After losing to Stephen Hendry in the Continental Airlines London Masters at the Café Royal, Steve Davis said: *"I was incredibly ordinary out there."*

"My problem is that I hit a peak at the start of the season and I've been struggling to match that." Steve Davis after losing to Stephen Hendry in the semi-final of the Benson and Hedges Masters at Wembley.

"9-4 was flattering; I played badly" Cliff Thorburn's comments after crashing out of the Everest World Match Play to Joe Johnson.

Memorable Match

Steve Davis v Jimmy White (Norwich Union European Grand Prix Final)

It is not often that Steve finds himself trailing 4-1 in a best-of-nine frame match, but in the Norwich Union European Grand Prix final in Monte Carlo in December that was his dilemma.

A low scoring sixth frame saw Steve win 40-30, and he won the next with a 60 break.

With only pink and black left in the eighth frame, Steve needed a snooker to save the match. Jimmy successfully escaped from three and then potted the pink for the match . . . only to see the white go in-off. Steve got the points he had been looking for, took the last two balls and won the frame 59-55. That made it four-all and in the final frame Steve won with a clearance of 35. A great comeback, even by his standards.

won the opening round in Brussels, Steve won in Paris, Jimmy in Madrid, and Terry won the final round in Milan. Those four then played off for the £50,000 first prize in Monte Carlo and in a memorable final Steve beat Jimmy 5-4 to take his season's winnings to £423,000.

The **Benson and Hedges Masters** at Wembley is the longest running of the current tournaments, after the World Championship, and the Wembley Conference Centre is snooker's biggest venue, capable of holding crowds in excess of 2,500.

Seven of the eight Matchroom players made the short trip to North London, only Tony Meo being missing. Another notable absentee, for the first time in 15 years, was Alex Higgins.

BIG CROWD FOR JIMMY AND JOHN

Two Matchroom men fell at the first hurdle; Dennis lost to John Parrott and Willie was ousted by Stephen Hendry. But Neal Foulds had his first Wembley success in three attempts when he beat Peter Francisco, and in the quarter-final he beat Cliff 5-2. Terry at this stage lost to Stephen Hendry and Jimmy lost a great battle with John Parrott that went its full distance. Their match was watched by 2,388 fans.

Steve beat Tony Knowles to get in the last four but Hendry made sure he didn't get his name on the trophy for the third time by playing magnificent snooker to beat the defending champion. In the other semi-final, Neal lost 6-5 to John Parrott.

The final was the first Masters without a Matchroom player since 1985, and the new champion was Hendry, who beat Parrott 9-6. For him there was a £68,000 cheque, but for Parrott it was his third consecutive defeat in a major final. ▶

MATCHROOM

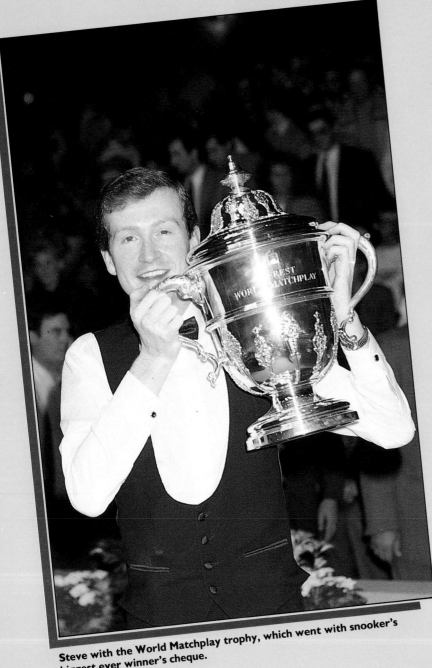

Steve with the World Matchplay trophy, which went with snooker's biggest ever winner's cheque.

Professional title for six years when he beat defending champion Jack McLaughlin 9-7 in the final. Like the English event, it was devalued because Ireland's top player, Dennis Taylor, did not compete.

The **Scottish Championship** was also without the country's top player, Stephen Hendry, and the title went to John Rea, who beat Murdo Mcleod 9-7 in the final. It was a memorable tournament for Rea, who compiled a 147 maximum in his quarter-final with Ian Black.

MATCHROOM'S WORLD CUP

Fersina Windows once more sponsored the **World Cup** at Bournemouth and for the second year running the Matchroom trio of Davis, Foulds and White lifted the title for England. But what a fright they got from the Rest of the World team of Silvino Francisco, Tony Drago and Dene O'Kane.

England seemed to be coasting to victory at 8-5, needing just one more frame for victory, but Drago and his skipper Francisco levelled the match at 8-all. The decider between Davis and O'Kane was a nail-biter which Steve managed to win after 73 minutes play and a re-spotted black.

If anybody still thinks the players don't care too much for this sort of tournament, they should have seen the anxious looks on the faces of the other four players as Davis and O'Kane battled it out for that final frame . . .

ALEX WINS AGAIN

Alex Higgins turned back the clock to win his first major tournament since the 1983 Coral UK Championship when he beat Stephen Hendry 9-8 to become the first Irish winner of the **Benson and Hedges Irish Masters.**

The partisan crowd willed on every one of Alex's shots as he came back from 5-2 in arrears at the interval. He also found himself trailing 8-6 but showed great character in beating his younger opponent. Higgins collected the first prize of

THE NATIONAL CHAMPIONSHIPS

Between the European Open and British Open, the four Home Counties staged their National Professional Championships.

The **English Championship** was considerably devalued with many top names missing the untelevised event, including Steve Davis.

Mike Hallett ended a 10-year wait for a major title when he beat John Parrott 9-7 in the final at Bristol. The two losing semi-finalists were Gary Wilkinson and our own Neal Foulds.

Terry Griffiths went one better than Neal by reaching the final of the **Welsh Professional Championship** at Newport but lost 9-6 to the "Man of the Season" Doug Mountjoy. Terry led 5-1 at one stage but Doug won eight of the next nine frames to clinch the title for the first time since 1984.

Alex Higgins won his first **Irish**

27,000 while the break prize went to Hendry for his 136.

Steve retained the Matchroom League title, losing only one of his nine matches, 6-2 to Jimmy in the last match of the season at Brentwood. The win was good enough to make sure the "Whirlwind" was not relegated. However, Alex Higgins and Terry Griffiths both lost their League places. During his 7-1 win over Jimmy White at Crawley Cliff Thorburn scored a 147 break, becoming the first to register two official maximums.

The last tournament of the season saw stable-mates Stephen Hendry and John Parrott contest the final of the Continental Airlines London Masters at the Café Royal in London. Hendry won 4-2. ■

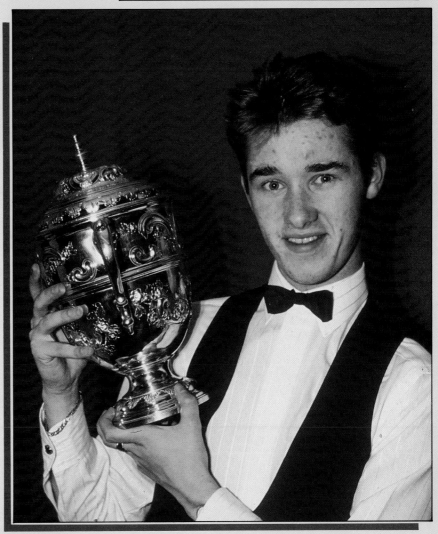

Young Master Hendry: Stephen with the Benson and Hedges Masters Trophy. He was the youngest to win this title.

WHO WON WHAT

Tournament	Winner	Score	Runner-up
Pontins Professional Champs:	John Parrott	9-1	Mike Hallett
New Zealand Masters:	Stephen Hendry	6-1	Mike Hallett
Fiat Snooker/Pool Triathlon:	Steve Mizarek	6-4	**Jimmy White**
LEP Hong Kong Masters:	**Jimmy White**	6-3	**Neal Foulds**
Australian Professional Champs:	John Campbell	9-7	Robbie Foldvari
Canadian Professional Champs:	Alain Robidoux	8-4	Jim Wych
WPBSA Tournament (1):	Gary Wilkinson	5-4	Alex Higgins
WPBSA Tournament (2):	Paddy Browne	5-1	Peter Francisco
Fosters Professional Champs:	Mike Hallett	8-5	Stephen Hendry
LEP Matchroom Champs:	**Steve Davis**	10-7	**Dennis Taylor**
Dubai Duty Free Masters:	**Neal Foulds**	5-4	**Steve Davis**
Everest World Match-Play:	**Steve Davis**	9-5	John Parrott
Norwich Union Grand Prix:	**Steve Davis**	5-4	**Jimmy White**
Benson & Hedges Masters:	Stephen Hendry	9-6	John Parrott
Fersina Windows World Cup:	England	9-8	Rest of the World
Benson & Hedges Irish Masters:	Alex Higgins	9-8	Stephen Hendry
Matchroom League:	**Steve Davis**		John Parrott
Continental Airline Masters:	Stephen Hendry	4-2	John Parrott

British and Best!

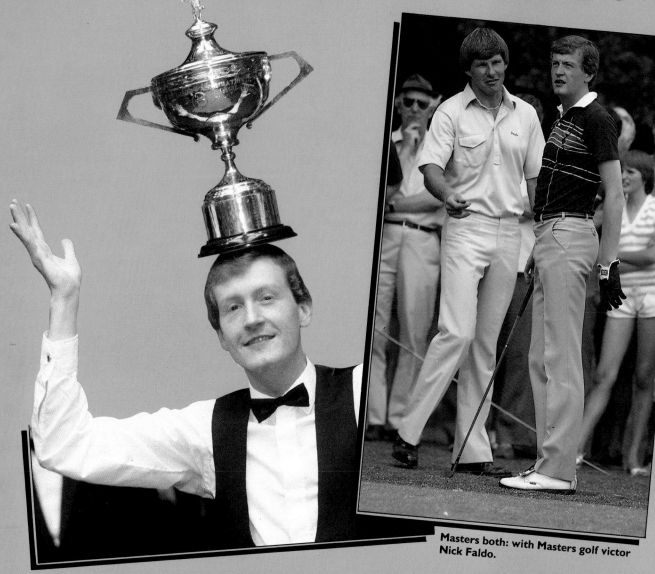

Masters both: with Masters golf victor Nick Faldo.

If only more British sportsmen and women had the same insatiable desire to win as Steve . . .

It was around Steve that Matchroom was built. Two years after teaming up with Barry in 1976, Steve turned professional. In 1980 he won his first major tournament, the Coral UK Championship at Preston, and Barry raced to hug him. A year later the celebrations were repeated as Steve became Champion of the World. Since then Steve has gone on winning . . . and winning.

TRIPLE WORLD CHAMPION

He has won nearly as many ranking tournaments as all other professionals between them, including the world title a Crucible record six times. In 1984 he laid the Crucible bogey by retaining his title, the first man to do so. After two consecutive defeats by Dennis Taylor, in that memorable black-ball final of 1985, and Joe Johnson a year later, Steve regained his title in 1987 and the following year beat Terry in an all-Matchroom contest. In 1989 he became the first man to win three consecutive Crucible titles when he defied all those pundits who had written him off (yet again!) by playing some of the finest snooker of his career to beat John Parrott 18-3; the biggest winning margin in Crucible history.

Steve has been labelled by some of the sensational papers as "boring", by which they mean: "consistently brilliant".

Steve Davis

Born Plumstead, London, 22 August 1957

◉ CAREER HIGHLIGHTS ◉

RANKING TOURNAMENTS

1981 Embassy World Professional Championship
1983 Embassy World Professional Championship, Jameson International
1984 Lada Classic, Embassy World Professional Championship, Jameson International, Coral UK Championship
1985 Rothmans Grand Prix, Coral UK Championship
1986 Dulux British Open, Tennents UK Championship
1987 Mercantile Credit Classic, Embassy World Professional Championship, Fidelity Unit Trusts International, Tennents UK Championship
1988 Mercantile Credit Classic, Embassy World Professional Championship, Fidelity Unit Trusts International, Rothmans Grand Prix
1989 Embassy World Professional Championship

OTHER TOURNAMENTS

1980 Coral UK Championship
1981 Yahama International Masters, Courage English Professional Championship, Jameson International, Coral UK Championship, State Express World Team Classic (member of England team)
1982 Benson and Hedges Masters, Yahama International Masters, Tolly Cobbold Classic, Langs Scottish Masters, Hofmeister World Doubles (with Tony Meo)
1983 Lada Classic, Tolly Cobbold Classic, Benson and Hedges Irish Masters, Langs Scottish Masters, State Express World Team Classic (member of England team), Hofmeister World Doubles (with Tony Meo)
1984 Benson and Hedges Irish Masters, Tolly Cobbold Classic, Langs Scottish Masters
1985 Tolly Cobbold English Professional Championship, Hofmeister World Doubles (with Tony Meo)
1986 Hofmeister World Doubles (with Tony Meo)
1987 Benson and Hedges Irish Masters
1988 Benson and Hedges Masters, Fersina World Cup (member of England team), Benson and Hedges Irish Masters, LEP Matchroom Championship, Everest World Match Play Championship, Norwich Union Grand Prix.
1989 Fersina Windows World Cup (member of England team), Matchroom League

1988-89 HIGHLIGHTS

Ranking Tournaments:
Fidelity Unit Trusts International:
Final beat Jimmy White 12-6
Rothmans Grand Prix:
Final beat Alex Higgins 10-6
BCE Canadian Masters:
Final lost Jimmy White 4-9
Tennents UK Championship:
Semi-final lost Stephen Hendry 3-9
Mercantile Credit Classic:
Round 3 lost Tony Chappel 3-5
ICI European Open
Did not play
Anglian British Open:
Quarter-final lost John Parrott 1-5
Embassy World Professional Championship:
Final beat John Parrott 18-3

The style which has taken Steve to the top of the world – six times.

Steve Davis
DID YOU KNOW?

- Steve was honoured with the MBE in the 1988 Birthday Honours List.
- Steve's debut at the Crucible was in 1979. His first opponent was current stablemate Dennis Taylor. Dennis won 13-11.
- Steve went a record 22 ranking matches without defeat in 1988. Jimmy White ended the run in the final of the Canadian Masters.
- Steve owns a forest in Scotland and a 200-acre farm near Romford.

MATCHROOM

Before 1989 Tony's successes were mostly at doubles with Steve.

NOT ONLY A DOUBLES MAN NOW

Tony joined the stable shortly before Matchroom was formed in 1982 and was the second member of the team. He had an outstanding record as a junior and had turned professional in 1979.

He and Steve joined forces for the inaugural World Doubles Championship in 1982 and scooped the first prize. They have since made the competition their own, winning it four times.

ROBBED BY AUDIENCE

Individual honours have often eluded Tony. In the 1984 Lada Classic he was on the verge of winning until a member of the audience spoilt his concentration and Steve won 9-8. But in 1986 Tony won his first major individual prize when he beat Neal Foulds to win the Tolly Cobbold English Professional Championship at Ipswich. A year later he retained his title.

Tony Meo

Born Hampstead, London, 4 October 1959

1989 COMEBACK

Tony started the 1988-89 season ranked 31 following a series of disastrous tournaments, but, out of the blue, he found his old confidence and surprised everybody to win the Anglian British Open at Derby.

He never looked back after a fifth round win over Stephen Hendry, and in the semi-final against Mike Hallett he showed great character to come from the brink of defeat and snatch a dramatic 9-8 win. In the final he disposed of Dean Reynolds 13-6 to take the £70,000 first prize. He then reached the World Championship semi-final, and aimed once more towards the top 16.

● CAREER HIGHLIGHTS ●

RANKING TOURNAMENTS

1984 Lada Classic (runner-up)
1989 Anglia British Open

OTHER TOURNAMENTS

1981 Winfield Masters
1982 Hofmeister World Doubles (with Steve Davis)
1983 Hofmeister World Doubles (with Steve Davis), State Express World Team Classic (member of England team)
1985 Winfield Masters, Hofmeister World Doubles (with Steve Davis)
1986 Tolly Cobbold English Professional Championship, Hofmeister World Doubles (with Steve Davis)
1987 Tolly Cobbold English Professional Championship

Tony Meo DID YOU KNOW?

- Tony Meo and Jimmy White used to be school mates. They both went to the Ernest Bevin Comprehensive School in Tooting . . . Tony attended a bit more often than Jimmy!
- Tony used to be managed by Henry West; the stable's top player at the time was Patsy Fagan.
- Playing Terry Whitthread in 1976 Tony compiled his first maximum break, at the age of 17 the youngest to do so.
- Tony was born in London of Italian parents. When he was 13 they decided to return to their native land. Tony had the choice of going to Italy or staying in London. Happily for the snooker world he stayed.
- Tony Meo is the Ian Botham of the snooker world .. when he can he slips away for a game of cricket.

1988-89 HIGHLIGHTS

Ranking Tournaments:
Fidelity Unit Trusts International:
Quarter-final lost Steve James 1-5
Rothmans Grand Prix:
Round 4 lost Alain Robidoux 0-5
BCE Canadian Masters:
Round 3 lost Marcel Gauvreau 0-5
Tennents UK Championship:
Round 3 lost David Roe 7-9
Mercantile Credit Classic:
Round 4 lost Silvino Francisco 1-5
ICI European Open:
Round 3 lost David Roe 1-5
Anglian British Open:
Final beat Dean Reynolds 13-6
Embassy World Professional Championship:
Semi-final lost John Parrott 7-16

Tony and wife Denise know how to enjoy life – but it looks too much for small daughter!

MATCHROOM

The Polished Pro.

GREAT BATTLES WITH STEVE

Terry was the third member of the Matchroom team, having joined in May 1982. He had the image that fitted the Barry Hearn organisation: polished, and with an excellent track record.

A former Welsh and English Amateur Champion, he turned professional in 1978 after failing to qualify for the World Amateur Championships in Malta. The move was fully justified: a year later Terry was the *Professional* Champion of the World! He beat Perrie Mans, Alex Higgins and Eddie Charlton (in a wonderful long drawn out semi-final), before beating current team-mate Dennis Taylor in the final.

From then on Terry became one of the toughest men to play and his battles with Steve in the early 1980s were memorable. Although Steve inflicted some heavy defeats on him, Terry beat Steve 9-8 in a great final to win the 1982 Lada Classic and 9-5 to win the Benson and Hedges Irish Masters later in the season. At the end of the year Terry triumphed in one of his finest matches when he squeezed past Alex Higgins 16-15 to win the Coral UK Championship.

Remarkably, Terry's only ranking success is that World Championship win in 1979. He has reached two other ranking finals, the 1988 World Championship, when he lost to Steve, and the inaugural ICI European Open in 1989 when he lost to first-time winner John Parrott 9-8.

Nevertheless since 1983 consistent Terry has never been out of the top ten.

Terry pulls another trick shot out of the bag – or, in this case, basket.

Terry Griffiths

Born Llanelli, 16 October 1947

• CAREER HIGHLIGHTS •

RANKING TOURNAMENTS

1979 Embassy World Professional Championship
1988 Embassy World Professional Championship
(runner-up)
1989 ICI European Open (runner-up)

OTHER TOURNAMENTS

1979 State Express World Team Classic (member
of Wales team)
1980 Benson and Hedges Masters, Benson and
Hedges Irish Masters, State Express World
Team Classic (member of Wales team)
1981 Benson and Hedges Irish Masters
1982 Lada Classic, Benson and Hedges Irish
Masters, Coral UK Championship
1985 Welsh Professional Championship
1986 Welsh Professional Championship, BCE
Belgian Classic
1988 Welsh Professional Championship

**Terry likes to study his next shot, whether
at snooker** (below) **or golf** (left).
**Unfortunately at golf he can't get the ball
and hole at eye level!**

1988-89 HIGHLIGHTS

Ranking Tournaments:
Fidelity Unit Trusts International:
Round 3 lost Jim Wych 0-5
Rothmans Grand Prix:
Quarter-final lost Steve Davis 3-5
BCE Canadian Masters:
Quarter-final lost Steve Davis 3-5
Tennents UK Championship:
Semi-final lost Doug Mountjoy 4-9
Mercantile Credit Classic:
Round 5 lost Willie Thorne 1-5
ICI European Open:
Final lost John Parrott 8-9
Anglian British Open:
Round 3 lost Mark Johnston-Allen 1-5
Embassy World Professional Championship:
Quarter-final lost Stephen Hendry 5-13

Terry Griffiths DID YOU KNOW?

- Of all the Matchroom men, Terry must surely have had the greatest variety of former jobs before he turned to professional snooker: he used to be a postman, bus conductor and insurance agent.
- In 1987 Terry opened his own 15-table snooker centre in his home town of Llanelli.
- Terry's son Wayne followed dad's footsteps by winning the Llanelli and District Championship in 1987. Terry was 16 when he won the title; Wayne was only 15. But Wayne has no plans to follow dad into the world of professional snooker. He plays for enjoyment only.
- Two of Terry's old schoolmates were Derek Quinnell and Phil Bennett; both went on to play Rugby Union for Wales.

Dennis's Taylor-Made GLASSES

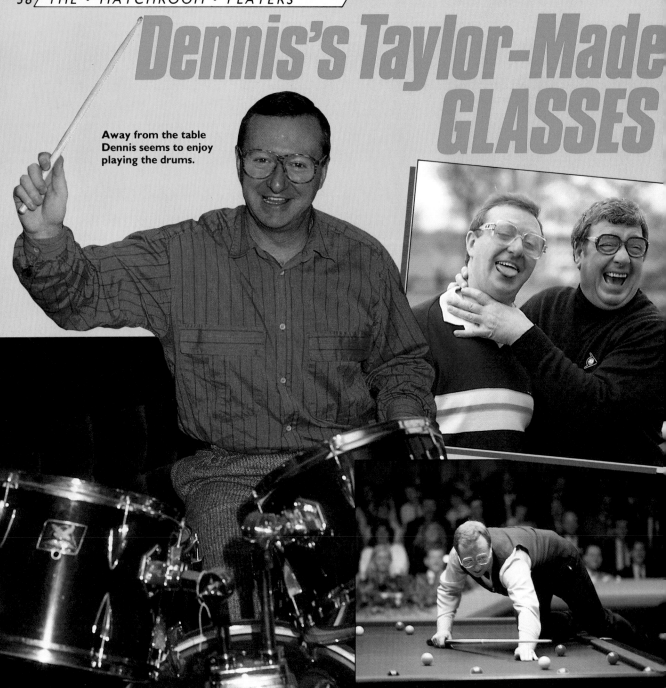

Away from the table Dennis seems to enjoy playing the drums.

Matchroom went three years as a three-man team, but when Dennis Taylor beat Steve in that tremendous World final in 1985, Barry had no hesitation in recruiting the popular Irishman as team-member number four.

Dennis, like the others, was the right type for Matchroom. By winning his first major tournament, the Rothmans Grand Prix, six months before the World title, he had proved he was a player to be rated highly – and one better to have on the team than against it!

'It's the way I choke 'em' says Frank Carson, with Dennis as victim, but Dennis gets his own laughs by climbing on the table during a match.

DENNIS'S LONG WAIT

Dennis displayed his snooker talent at an early age at Joe Girvan's snooker hall in Coalisland, and to develop his talents further he came to Blackburn as a 17-year-old. He turned professional in 1972: 12 years was a long wait for his first major win.

Dennis Taylor

Born Coalisland, Co. Tyrone, Northern Ireland, 19 January 1949

As a Matchroom member Dennis reached his second successive Rothmans final in 1985 but Steve beat him 0-9. Two years later he was the beaten finalist again, when Stephen Hendry won his first ranking tournament.

In his first year at Matchroom Dennis moved up from fourth to third in the world. He has slipped slightly since but is still very much a man to beat.

● CAREER HIGHLIGHTS ●

RANKING TOURNAMENTS

1979 Embassy World Professional Championship (runner up)
1984 Rothmans Grand Prix
1985 Embassy World Professional Championship, Rothmans Grand Prix (runner-up)
1987 Rothmans Grand Prix (runner-up)

OTHER TOURNAMENTS

1982 Irish Professional Championship; Guinness World Cup (member of All-Ireland team), Irish Professional Championship, BCE Canadian Masters, Kit Kat Break for Champions
1986 Car Care Plan World Cup (member of Ireland 'A' team), Irish Professional Championship, Carlsberg Challenge
1987 Tuborg World Cup (member of Ireland 'A' team), Benson and Hedges Masters, Irish Professional Championship, Carling Challenge

1988-89 HIGHLIGHTS

Ranking Tournaments:
Fidelity Unit Trusts International:
Quarter-final lost Steve Davis 2-5
Rothmans Grand Prix
Semi-final lost Steve Davis 1-9
BCE Canadian Masters:
Quarter-final lost Jimmy White 3-5
Tennents UK Championship:
Round 5 lost John Parrott 4-9
Mercantile Credit Classic:
Round 4 lost Steve Newbury 4-5
ICI European Open:
Round 4 lost Doug Mountjoy 3-5
Anglian British Open:
Round 3 lost Colin Roscoe 4-5
Embassy World Professional Championship:
Round 2 lost John Parrott 10-13

Dennis Taylor
DID YOU KNOW?

◉ Dennis used to live in a house in the middle of Blackburn golf course.
◉ Dennis is famous for his 'Joe 90' spectacles. But did you know they made their 'debut' at the 1983 Benson and Hedges Irish Masters? Some wag pointed out that they 'looked like a pair of Ford Cortina headlights'.
◉ The Dennis Taylor – Steve Davis World Championship final in 1985 attracted a television audience of 18½ million, the biggest for a sporting event in Britain.
◉ Dennis' pet terrier Chalkie was not the most popular of dogs in the Blackburn area in 1987. He chewed the end of the cue which won Dennis the world title.
◉ Back home in Coalisland as a junior, Dennis was so good that none of the locals would play him. In order to get a game Dennis had to play left-handed.

Surely Willie wouldn't have the nerve to smile at Dennis's haircut?

MATCHROOM

MATCHROOM'S MAXIMUM MAN

As a youngster Willie Thorne was the most successful of all eight players who as professionals joined Matchroom. He won six junior titles at billiards and snooker between 1971-73 and in 1975 made the decision to turn professional.

Despite his dedication he could not challenge the domination of such men as Ray Reardon, John Spencer and Alex Higgins. But in 1984, after a good run in the World Championships two years earlier, Willie at last broke into the top 16 and began to show his true merit. With his good friend Cliff Thorburn, he reached the final of the 1984 World Doubles Championship, but they lost to Jimmy White and Alex Higgins.

WILLIE BREAKS THROUGH

But Willie's finest hour was not far away. Before the 1984-85 season was over, he had his hands on his first major title, the Mercantile Credit Classic. After beating Steve Davis 9-8 in a thrilling semi-final, Willie beat his mate Cliff 13-8 in the final.

In February 1986, Willie became the fifth member of Matchroom stable and shortly afterwards reached the Dulux British Open final, but lost 12-7 to Steve.

Willie and the Matchroom Trophy and (far right) **on the golf links.**

Willie Thorne

Born Leicester, 4 March 1954

Willie is snooker's champion break builder. He has nearly 100 maximums to his credit, all but one being in practice matches. The one that counted was against Tommy Murphy in the fourth round of the 1987 Tennents UK Championship.

● CAREER HIGHLIGHTS ●

RANKING TOURNAMENTS

1985 Mercantile Credit Classic, Coral UK Championship (runner-up)
1986 Dulux British Open (runner-up)

OTHER TOURNAMENTS

1984 Hofmeister World Doubles (runner-up with Cliff Thorburn)
1986 Matchroom Trophy

1988-89 HIGHLIGHTS

Ranking Tournaments:
Fidelity Unit Trusts International:
Round 5 lost Jimmy White 4-5
Rothmans Grand Prix:
Round 3 lost Gary Wilkinson 2-5
BCE Canadian Masters:
Round 4 lost Doug Mountjoy 4-5
Tennents UK Championship:
Round 5 lost Stephen Hendry 4-9
Mercantile Credit Classic:
Semi-final lost Wayne Jones 4-9
ICI European Open:
Round 5 lost Jimmy White 3-5
Anglian British Open:
Round 5 lost Steve Davis 0-5
Embassy World Professional Championship:
Round 2 lost Stephen Hendry 4-13

Willie Thorne
DID YOU KNOW?

● One of Willie's maximum breaks came in 1982 when he had both legs in plaster following a go-karting accident.
● Playing Murdo McLeod in the 1982 Professional Players' Tournament Willie compiled breaks of 94, 109 and 135 in consecutive frames – but lost the match 5-4!
● One of Willie's best friends is Barcelona and England soccer star Gary Lineker. Gary's a bit better at snooker than Willie is at soccer. The goalscoring ace has knocked in a few century breaks in his time.
● When Willie compiled his only 147 break in tournament play it was in the non-televised stage of the 1987 Tennents UK Championship. Had it been one round later the feat would have earned Willie £50,000 . . . as it was he collected £6,750.

Willie and pals – *(left)* **Cliff, very smart at Willie's wedding, and** *(right)* **Gary Lineker potting a few at Willie's club.**

MATCHROOM

NEAL RISES

Neal with the BCE International, his first major trophy, and proud dad Geoff.

NEAL'S FINE RUN

In 1986 Neal Foulds had the opportunity of becoming Mark McCormack's first snooker player on the books of the International Management Group, but he joined Matchroom instead.

Neal turned professional in 1983. When he joined Matchroom he was number 13 in the world. A year later he was number three behind Steve and Jimmy.

He first attracted attention when he beat Alex Higgins on his Crucible debut in the 1984 World Championship. He reached his first major final in the 1986 English Professional Championship but lost 9-7 to Tony Meo. Shortly afterwards Neal teamed up with Matchroom.

He opened the next season by beating Cliff 12-9 to win the BCE International at Stoke. He then reached the final of the Coral UK Championship but lost 16-7 to Steve. He reached his third ranking final but lost to Jimmy in the Dulux British Open, then reached the semi-final of the World Championship – enough to rise to number three in the rankings.

He consolidated in 1987-88 but then struggled, while off-the-table problems did not help. However, he played some of his best snooker for a long time in beating Cliff, Tony and Steve to collect the £25,000 winner's cheque in the Dubai Duty Free Masters in 1988-89.

Neal Foulds

Born Perivale, Middlesex, 13 July 1963

Neal Foulds
DID YOU KNOW?

- Neal's dad Geoff is also a professional player and expert coach. Geoff was the technical adviser for the BBC television series *Give Us a Break* in 1983 and actually played most of the shots off camera.
- Neal and his dad Geoff twice met each other in major tournament play in 1986. Neal won both times, the second a 5-0 "whitewash" . . . there's gratitude for you!
- Neal used to wear spectacles but after switching to contact lenses when he was 16 his form on the snooker table improved.
- Neal is the proud owner of several greyhounds, the best being Greenfield Game. All are prefixed with the word 'Greenfield' and are trained at Windsor by Les Dickson.
- Neal has another sporting love – cricket. In the summer months he enjoys nothing more than packing a picnic and enjoying it at Lord's watching Middlesex.

Neal posing with his father Geoff, who, of course, was a big influence on his game, coaching him from a youngster.

CAREER HIGHLIGHTS

RANKING TOURNAMENTS

1986 BCE International, Tennents UK Open (runner-up)
1987 Dulux British Open (runner-up)

OTHER TOURNAMENTS

1988 Fersina Windows World Cup (member of England team), Dubai Duty Free Masters
1989 Fersina Windows World Cup (member of England team)

1988-89 HIGHLIGHTS

Ranking Tournaments:
Fidelity Unit Trusts International:
Round 4 lost Dean Reynolds 3-5
Rothmans Grand Prix:
Round 5 lost Alex Higgins 3-5
BCE Canadian Masters:
Round 3 lost Warren King 3-5
Tennents UK Championship:
Round 4 lost Doug Mountjoy 4-9
Mercantile Credit Classic:
Round 4 lost Martin Clark 4-5
ICI European Open:
Round 3 lost Martin Clark 3-5
Anglian British Open:
Round 5 lost Martin Clark 4-5
Embassy World Professional Championship:
Round 1 lost Wayne Jones 9-10

MATCHROOM

A team that claims to be the strongest must contain the best players in the world. And a snooker team without Jimmy White cannot rightly make such a claim. That is why the tempestuous but brilliant White made Matchroom the "Magnificent Seven" in September 1986.

One of the game's finest potters, White's trademark is his speed around the table, hence his nickname, "Whirlwind". Jimmy won the World Amateur Championship in 1980 and turned professional on his return from Tasmania. He became the youngest winner of a professional tournament in 1981 when he won the Langs Scottish Masters, and then he beat World Champion Steve Davis to win the Northern Ireland Classic. Not bad for a 19-year-old!

JIMMY FIGHTS BACK

A lean period must have made Jimmy wonder, but victory in the Benson and Hedges Masters re-confirmed him as a winner in 1984. A couple of months later he went all the way to the final of the World Championship at Sheffield, where he lost a terrific battle with Steve by 18-16.

Jimmy won his first ranking tournament in 1986 when he beat Cliff 13-12 in the Mercantile Credit Classic. Since then Jimmy has won the Rothmans Grand Prix and BCE Canadian Masters and has maintained a ranking high among the world's top players.

⚫ CAREER HIGHLIGHTS ⚫

RANKING TOURNAMENTS

1982 Professional Players' Tournament (runner-up)
1984 Embassy World Professional Championship (runner-up)
1985 Goya Matchroom Trophy (runner-up)
1986 Mercantile Credit Classic, Rothmans Grand Prix
1987 Mercantile Credit Classic (runner-up), Tennents UK Championship (runner-up), Dulux British Open
1988 Fidelity Unit Trusts International (runner-up), BCE Canadian Masters

A WELL-SCHOOLED TALENT

Jimmy White

Born Tooting, London, 2 May 1962

OTHER TOURNAMENTS

1980 World Amateur Championship
1981 Langs Scottish Masters, Northern Ireland Classic
1984 Benson and Hedges Masters, Carlsberg Challenge
1985 Benson and Hedges Irish Masters, Carlsberg Challenge
1986 Benson and Hedges Irish Masters
1988 Fersina Windows World Cup (member of England team)

1988-89 HIGHLIGHTS

Ranking Tournaments:
Fidelity Unit Trusts International:
Final lost Steve Davis 6-12
Rothmans Grand Prix:
Quarter-final lost Dennis Taylor 2-5
BCE Canadian Masters:
Final beat Steve Davis 9-4
Tennents UK Championship:
Round 4 lost Mark Bennett 6-9
Mercantile Credit Classic:
Round 3 lost Wayne Jones 3-5
ICI European Open:
Semi-final lost Terry Griffiths 4-5
Anglian British Open:
Round 4 scratched
Embassy World Professional Championship:
Quarter-final lost John Parrott 7-13

Jimmy White DID YOU KNOW?

- Jimmy used to attend (sometimes!) the Ernest Bevin School in Tooting but was more intent on playing snooker at Zans Snooker Hall. Headmaster Mr Beattie made a deal with the youngster after realising how good Jimmy was. "Come to school in the morning and play snooker in the afternoon" was the deal. Jimmy obliged . . . and look where it got him!
- After winning the 1980 World Amateur crown in Tasmania, Jimmy stopped off in India to take part in their national amateur championship. He won that as well!
- When Jimmy became the seventh member of Matchroom in 1986 he paid £50,000 to be bought out of his contract with his previous management team.

Jimmy in three of his guises. *Opposite page* **As the fans know him, fast and deadly on the table.** *Left* **Fighting a mock duel with Steve Davis, to whom he was number two in the world.** *Above* **Relaxing with wife Maureen.**

MATCHROOM

LATE~ NIGHT CLIFF~ HANGER

Cliff's is one of the best-known faces on the snooker circuit, but he sometimes says he prefers golf – he is an excellent player.

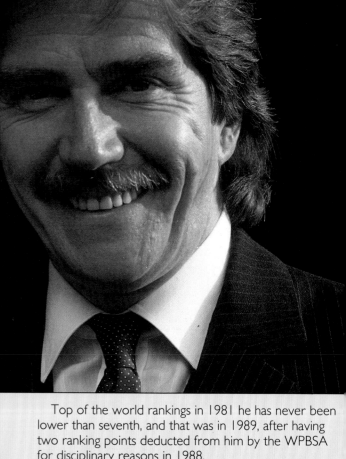

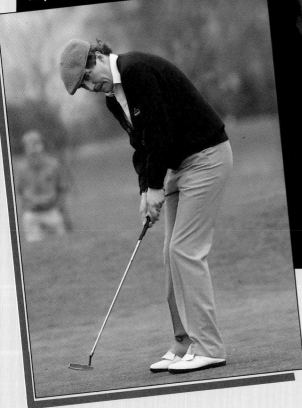

Top of the world rankings in 1981 he has never been lower than seventh, and that was in 1989, after having two ranking points deducted from him by the WPBSA for disciplinary reasons in 1988.

GOING THE DISTANCE

The finest ever Canadian snooker player Cliff reached his first World final in 1977 when he lost to John Spencer. It was the first final at the Crucible. His other losing final was against Steve Davis in 1983. Cliff lost 18-6, but was drained after his three previous matches had all gone the full distance, lasting until the small hours.

Cliff has appeared in seven other ranking finals, but has won only one, against Jimmy White in the 1985 Goya International. Since teaming up with Steve and the rest of the boys he hasn't yet reached a ranking final, but one cannot be too far away.

When Cliff joined Matchroom at the beginning of 1988 he relieved Dennis Taylor of one tag . . . that of oldest member of the playing squad! Three times a World finalist, Cliff won the title in 1980 when he beat Alex Higgins in an enthralling final. Since then he has been one of the most consistent players in the world and is acknowledged as just about the toughest competitor on the circuit.

Cliff Thorburn

Born Victoria, British Columbia, Canada, 16 January 1948

● CAREER HIGHLIGHTS ●

RANKING TOURNAMENTS

1977 Embassy World Professional Championship (runner-up)
1980 Embassy World Professional Championship
1983 Embassy World Professional Championship (runner-up), Jameson International (runner-up)
1984 Rothmans Grand Prix (runner-up)
1985 Mercantile Credit Classic (runner-up), Goya Matchroom Trophy
1986 Mercantile Credit Classic (runner-up), BCE International (runner-up)
1987 Fidelity Unit Trusts International (runner-up)

OTHER TOURNAMENTS

1982 State Express World Team Classic (member of the Canada team)
1983 Benson and Hedges Masters, Winfield Masters
1985 Benson and Hedges Masters, Canadian Professional Championship, Langs Scottish Masters
1986 Benson and Hedges Masters, Canadian Professional Championship, Langs Scottish Masters

1988-89 HIGHLIGHTS

Ranking Tournaments:
Fidelity Unit Trusts International:
Did not play
Rothmans Grand Prix:
Did not play
BCE Canadian Masters:
Quarter-final lost Stephen Hendry 4-5
Tennents UK Championship:
Quarter-final lost Stephen Hendry 2-9
Mercantile Credit Classic:
Semi-final lost Doug Mountjoy 5-9
ICI European Open:
Quarter-final lost Jimmy White 3-5
Anglian British Open:
Round 5 lost Mike Hallett 4-5

Embassy World Professional Championship:
Round 1 lost Eddie Charlton 9-10

Cliff Thorburn
DID YOU KNOW?

● Like many snooker players Cliff is an expert golfer, and one of many who play to a single-figure handicap.
● Cliff lost 18-6 to Steve in the 1983 World Championship final. It is hardly surprising he lost because his three previous matches all went the maximum distance, a total of 81 frames. His second round match against Terry Griffiths lasted 6hr 25min and finished at 3.51am. His quarter-final against Kirk Stevens lasted 6hr 11min and finished at 2.12am, while his semi-final against Tony Knowles lasted a mere 4hr 45min and finished at 12.45am.
● Cliff's first professional match in England was against Dennis Taylor in the 1973 World Championship. Cliff won 9-8.
● Cliff is the only man to have compiled a maximum 147 in the World Championship. He did it while playing Terry Griffiths on 23 April 1983, and began with a fluked red!
● Steve Davis was not the first Matchroom member to receive a decoration. Cliff was awarded Order of Canada (CM) in 1984.

Cliff among the balls. He is the only player to make two 147 maximums in tournament play.

MATCHROOM

The Steve 'n' Stephen Shows

Stephen Hendry beat Steve Davis three times during the season, but lost to him in the World semi-final

QUOTES...
FROM MATCHROOM PLAYERS

"That was heavy artillery from him today" Steve Davis about Stephen Hendry's 9-3 win in their semi-final clash in the 1988 Tennents UK Championship

U ndoubtedly the biggest threat to the Matchroom domination comes from the Scot Stephen Hendry. Still only 20, he has risen from number 51 in the world to become one of Steve's biggest challengers, and in just four years.

INFANT GENIUS

A dedicated professional, he was the national Under-16 Champion at the age of 14, and after twice winning the Scottish Amateur title he became the sport's youngest professional in 1985 at the age of 16.

Scottish Professional Champion in his first season, he won his first ranking tournament, the 1987 Rothmans, when he beat Dennis Taylor 10-7 in the final. Since then he has added the British Open and the Benson and Hedges Masters.

Our own Steve has been involved in some great clashes with Hendry and while he has had the upper hand, the young Scot got the better of him on the way to winning the Rothmans, and again in the Tennents and Benson and Hedges Masters in 1988-89.

● CAREER HIGHLIGHTS ●

RANKING TOURNAMENTS

1987 Rothmans Grand Prix
1988 MIM Britannia British Open, Tennents UK Championship (runner-up)

Other Tournaments

1986 Scottish Professional Championship
1987 Scottish Professional Championship, Winfield Masters, Fosters World Doubles (with Mike Hallett)
1988 New Zealand Masters
1989 Benson and Hedges Masters

1988-89 HIGHLIGHTS

Ranking Tournaments:
Fidelity Unit Trusts International
Round 5 lost Steve James 2-5
Rothmans Grand Prix
Round 4 lost Doug Mountjoy 1-5
BCE Canadian Masters
Semi-final lost Steve Davis 5-9
Tennents UK Championship:
Final lost Doug Mountjoy 12-16
Mercantile Credit Classic
Quarter-final lost Cliff Thorburn 4-5
ICI European Open:
Round 5 lost Mike Hallett 3-5
Anglian British Open:
Round 5 lost Tony Meo 3-5
Embassy World Professional Championship:
Semi-final lost Steve Davis 9-16

Stephen Hendry   *Born Edinburgh, 13 January 1969*

THE EUROPEAN CHAMPION

Still only 25, John Parrott seems to have been around the professional scene a long time and is almost regarded as an "old-timer". He is a big danger to Steve's number one spot.

He first made his mark as a professional in the 1984 Lada Classic at Warrington when he beat Alex Higgins 5-2 and Tony Knowles 5-1 before engaging in a great battle with Steve Davis. He almost won, but Steve recovered to snatch a 5-4 semi-final victory.

NEAT DRESSER, NEAT PLAYER

Well dressed and well mannered, John has been a consistent performer ever since, and he broke into the top 16 in 1987.

He lost 13-11 to Steve in the final of the 1988 Mercantile Credit Classic, his first ranking final. Defeats by Steve in the inaugural Everest World Match Play in 1988 and by team-mate Stephen Hendry in the 1989 Benson and Hedges Masters must have left him wondering if he was ever going to win a major, but it all came right at Deauville when he beat Terry Griffiths 9-8 to win the first ICI European Open.

When humorist John Parrott met a namesake it seemed a good cue for a joke and a photo.

● CAREER HIGHLIGHTS ●

RANKING TOURNAMENTS

1988 Mercantile Credit Classic (runner-up)
1989 ICI European Open, Embassy World Professional Championship (runner-up)

OTHER TOURNAMENTS

1982 Pontins Open, Junior *Pot Black*
1983 Junior *Pot Black*
1988 Pontins Professional, Everest World Match Play (runner-up)
1989 Benson and Hedges Masters (runner-up)

1988-89 HIGHLIGHTS

Ranking Tournaments:
Fidelity Unit Trusts International:
Round 3 lost Les Dodd 4-5
Rothmans Grand Prix:
Round 4 lost Ray Edmonds 3-5
BCE Canadian Masters:
Quarter-final lost Mike Hallett 3-5
Tennents UK Championship:
Quarter-final lost Steve Davis 4-9
Mercantile Credit Classic:
Quarter-final lost Wayne Jones 4-5
ICI European Open:
Final beat Terry Griffiths 9-8
Anglian British Open:
Semi-final lost Dean Reynolds 8-9
Embassy World Professional Championship:
Final lost Steve Davis 3-18

John Parrott   *Born Liverpool, 11 May 1964*

MATCHROOM

THE HURRICANE BLOWS AGAIN!

The Hurricane on the course *(left)* and on the tab...

If this annual had appeared 12 months earlier, the name of Alex Higgins might not have appeared. But re-found success in 1988-89 marks him as a Matchroom rival.

It was at the Hexagon Theatre that we saw the Alex of old as he came through some nervous matches to meet Steve Davis in the final of the Rothmans Grand Prix. Alex was no match for Steve in the final, but in this youngster's age it was refreshing to see an "old-timer" star. And if Alex can do it once, he can do it again.

HEADLINE MAKER

He first hit the headlines in 1972 when, as a brash youngster, he won the world title by beating John Spencer. Ten years later he recaptured the crown when he beat Ray Reardon at Sheffield. Alex's last major individual championship success was the 1983 Coral UK Championship when he beat Steve 16-15 in one of the game's finest matches. Since then he has slid down the rankings, and the once legendary Davis-Higgins clashes have been one-sided affairs.

● CAREER HIGHLIGHTS ●

RANKING TOURNAMENTS

1976 Embassy World Professional Championship (runner-up)
1980 Embassy World Professional Championship (runner-up)
1982 Embassy World Professional Championship
1984 Coral UK Championship (runner-up)
1988 Rothmans Grand Prix (runner-up)

OTHER TOURNAMENTS

1972 World Professional Championship
1978 Benson and Hedges Masters
1980 British Gold Cup
1981 Benson and Hedges Masters
1983 Irish Professional Championship, Coral UK Championship
1984 Hofmeister World Doubles (with Jimmy White)
1985 World Cup (Member of All-Ireland team)
1986 World Cup (member of Ireland 'A' team)
1987 World Cup (member of Ireland 'A' team)
1989 Benson and Hedges Irish Masters, Irish Professional Championship

1988-89 HIGHLIGHTS

Ranking Tournaments:
Fidelity Unit Trusts International:
Round 3 lost Murdo McLeod 2-5
Rothmans Grand Prix:
Final lost Steve Davis 6-10
BCE Canadian Masters:
Round 3 lost Martin Clark 3-5
Tennents UK Championship:
Round 4 lost Tony Knowles 6-9
Mercantile Credit Classic:
Round 4 lost Joe Johnson 0-5
ICI European Open:
Round 4 lost Willie Thorne 1-5
Anglian British Open:
Round 4 lost Steve Davis 0-5
Embassy World Professional Championship:
Qualifying lost Darren Morgan 8-10

Alex Higgins

Born Belfast, 18 March 1949

Steve's Shocker

Although it is six years since Tony Knowles won a ranking tournament, he has kept his position in the top 16, and remained a scourge of the Matchroom men since the day he beat Steve 10-1 in the first round of the 1982 World Championship at Sheffield. That shock served notice that Tony was ready to take over Steve's crown. He never quite made it, but came close in 1984 when he was ranked number two in the world.

THREE TIMES SEMI-FINALIST

Tony was twice the Under-19 Champion before being accepted as a professional in 1980. He enjoyed his first major success in 1982 when he beat David Taylor 9-6 to win the Jameson International. The following year he reached the World Championship semi-final (the first of three times he has reached the last four), was in the England team that won the World Cup, and beat Joe Johnson to win the Professional Players' Tournament at Bristol.

That was Tony's last major success. But he is always a tough opponent, respected by even the best of the Matchroom men.

● CAREER HIGHLIGHTS ●

RANKING TOURNAMENTS

1982 Jameson International
1983 Professional Players' Tournament
1984 Jameson International (runner-up)

OTHER TOURNAMENTS

1983 World Cup (member of England team)
1984 Winfield Masters

1988-89 HIGHLIGHTS

Ranking Tournaments:
Fidelity Unit Trusts International:
Round 4 lost Steve Newbury 4-5
Rothmans Grand Prix:
Round 5 lost Nigel Gilbert 4-5
BCE Canadian Masters:
Round 3 lost Colin Roscoe 2-5
Tennents UK Championship:
Round 5 lost John Virgo 3-9
Mercantile Credit Classic:
Round 5 lost Doug Mountjoy 4-5
ICI European Open:
Round 3 lost Danny Fowler 2-5
Anglian British Open:
Round 4 lost Barry West 0-5
Embassy World Professional Championship:
Round 1 lost David Roe 6-10

Tony is as active out of doors as in. On the right, a delicate golf shot; on the left, more energetic water-skiing.

Tony Knowles

Born Bolton, 13 June 1955

MATCHROOM

For the success story of 1988-89 – step forward Doug Mountjoy. The 1976 World Amateur Champion, Welshman Doug turned professional, and in his first event, the 1977 Benson and Hedges Masters, he beat former World Champions Alex Higgins and Ray Reardon to win.

He then reached the final of the inaugural UK Championship but lost to Patsy Fagan. A year later he was Champion after beating David Taylor. In 1981 Doug was runner-up when Steve Davis won his first World title.

A NEW LEASE OF LIFE

But chapter two in the remarkable career of Doug Mountjoy was written in 1988. Without a major win since the 1978 Coral UK title, and slipping down the rankings, he sought advice from snooker *guru* Frank Callan. Frank's magic worked and 46-year-old Mountjoy was UK Champion again, after a break of ten years! He beat Stephen Hendry in the final and then went to Blackpool for the Mercantile Credit Classic and beat Wayne Jones in the final to become only the second man (after Steve) to win back-to-back ranking tournaments. A player who can do that is a serious threat to anybody, and Doug has to be taken very seriously now every time he picks up his cue.

● CAREER HIGHLIGHTS ●

RANKING TOURNAMENTS

1981 Embassy World Professional Championship (runner-up)
1988 Tennents UK Championship
1989 Mercantile Credit Classic

OTHER TOURNAMENTS

1976 World Amateur Championship
1977 Benson and Hedges Masters
1978 Coral UK Championship, Benson and Hedges Irish Masters, World Cup (member of Wales team)
1980 Welsh Professional Championship, World Cup (member of Wales team)
1982 Welsh Professional Championship
1984 Welsh Professional Championship
1987 Welsh Professional Championship
1989 Welsh Professional Championship

1988-89 HIGHLIGHTS

Ranking Tournaments:
Fidelity Unit Trusts International:
Round 4 lost Joe Johnson 4-5
Rothmans Grand Prix:
Round 5 lost Alain Robidoux 4-5
BCE Canadian Masters:
Round 5 lost Terry Griffiths 4-5
Tennents UK Championship:
Final beat Stephen Hendry 16-12
Mercantile Credit Classic:
Final beat Wayne Jones 13-11
ICI European Open:
Round 5 lost Cliff Thorburn 0-5
Anglian British Open:
Round 5 lost John Parrott 2-5
Embassy World Professional Championship:
Round 1 lost Mike Hallett 7-10

FORTIFYING THE OVER FORTIES

Doug Mountjoy won his first ranking tournaments in 1988-89.

> "I can never repay Frank (Callan) for what he's done for me"...
> Doug Mountjoy 1988

Doug Mountjoy Born Tir-y-Berth, Glamorgan, 8 June I

The singer with the group 'Made in Japan' is also quite a useful snooker player.

● CAREER HIGHLIGHTS ●

RANKING TOURNAMENTS

1986 Embassy World Professional Championship
1987 Embassy World Professional Championship (runner-up)

OTHER TOURNAMENTS

1978 World Amateur Championship (runner-up)
1987 Langs Scottish Masters

1988-89 HIGHLIGHTS

Ranking Tournaments:
Fidelity Unit Trusts International:
Quarter-final lost Dean Reynolds 1-5
Rothmans Grand Prix:
Round 4 lost Eugene Hughes 2-5
BCE Canadian Masters:
Round 4 lost Steve James 4-5
Tennents UK Championship:
Round 5 lost Doug Mountjoy 5-9
Mercantile Credit Classic:
Round 5 lost Martin Clark 4-5
ICI European Open:
Round 5 lost Martin Clark 8-9
Anglian British Open:
Quarter-final lost Dean Reynolds 4-5
Embassy World Professional Championship:
Round 1 lost Tony Meo 5-10

JOE'S CUE FOR A SONG

Joe wore spectacles for the 1988-89 season.

Joe Johnson has *always* been a good player, whose handicap seemed to be lack of confidence. However, in the 1986 World Championship final he oozed confidence as he beat Steve Davis.

Joe was runner-up to Cliff Wilson in the 1978 World Amateur Championship in Malta and turned professional a year later. He had never won a major professional honour until that World Championship, in which he knocked out Dave Martin, Mike Hallett, Terry Griffiths (a great match that ended 13-12) and Tony Knowles.

THE SINGING SNOOKER STAR

Next season reaction set in for happy-go-lucky Joe, and there was a run of one defeat after another. But when Crucible time came around Joe put up an inspired defence and reached the final again – but this time it was revenge for Steve.

Surprisingly these are Joe's only two ranking finals, but he remains among the elite of the snooker world. Away from the table Joe loves singing and has fronted with the Preston-based band 'Made in Japan'.

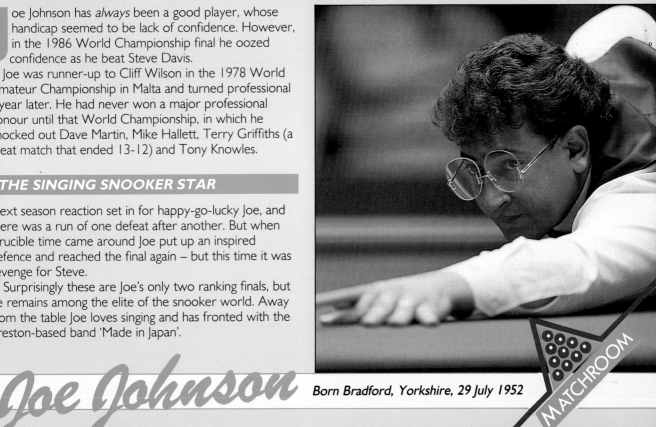

Joe Johnson

Born Bradford, Yorkshire, 29 July 1952

MATCHROOM

THE TEAM BEHIND THE TEAM

THE MATCHROOM TEAM

Matchroom is the biggest name in snooker. Having the best players in the world certainly helps, but any successful team consists of more than just the men out in the limelight. Matchroom is no exception.

But first of all, how did it all start?

Above **Some of the Matchroom boys in relaxed mood with some of the trophies they'd won.**
From left: **Willie, Dennis, Steve, Tony, Barry Hearn, Terry and Neal.**

Right: **Barry talks to the team in the office. Of the current Matchroom eight, Cliff and Jimmy are absent.**

THE LUCANIA CONNECTION

Barry Hearn's first involvement in snooker came in the 1970s when his company acquired the Lucania snooker halls, an old established chain of billiard halls that had been thriving since just after the First World War.

Barry, an accountant with the company, was based at the Romford branch of Lucania and in March 1976 his life changed dramatically. Because it was then that he set his eyes on

Steve Davis for the first time.

The tall ginger-haired youngster came to play at the Lucania Hall and his skills were brought to Barry's attention.

Having helped players like Geoff Foulds, Vic Harris and many other local amateurs with sponsorship, Barry immediately realised the potential of Davis and signed him up. One of sport's great partnerships was born. But Matchroom came later. In May 1982 Hearn sold 16 of 17 Lucania halls. The one he retained

was at Romford and the matchroom, where top players came to play Hearn's lads, was turned into a plush and separate part of the Lucania Hall (which still exists today with a membership of over 2,000).

MATCHROOM IS FORMED

After the sell-out of Lucania, a new company, Matchroom, was formed and the first two players under their control were Steve and Tony Meo, who had joined Barry's team in 1981. Terry Griffiths was recruited a month after the formation of Matchroom and since then Dennis Taylor, Willie Thorne, Neal Foulds, Jimmy White and Cliff Thorburn have made the team the strongest and most feared in the world of snooker.

THE BACKROOM OF MATCHROOM

But behind those eight great players lies another winning team; the administrators.

Barry, of course, is at the helm, but with a strong team behind him. Steve Dawson, his right-hand man, is financial director, and controls the large sums of money which come into (and go out of!) the Matchroom offices in Romford.

A team of girls play an important role – there are cheques to be written out, promotional material to distribute, countless fans who ask to meet Steve or the rest of the boys.

One of the most important members of the backroom team is "Robbo" (Brazier), chauffeur and "minder" to the eight players. A great character, Robbo spends as much time with the players as any of the Matchroom team, out on the road with them.

FROM POTS TO PUNCHES

Matchroom has diversified in the last couple of years and Barry has taken snooker's most famous name into boxing. The company's old offices have been converted into one of the most modern gymnasiums (Barry is a keep-fit fanatic himself).

On the books of the Matchroom boxing team is heavyweight Jess Harding. Barry won't be content until he has turned him into a champion, and Matchroom is number one in both snooker and boxing.

WHAT THE MATCHROOM MEN WON IN 1988-89

LEP Hong Kong Masters:	Jimmy White
Fidelity Unit Trusts International:	Steve Davis
Rothmans Grand Prix:	Steve Davis
BCE Canadian Masters:	Jimmy White
LEP Matchroom Championship:	Steve Davis
Dubai Duty Free Masters:	Neal Foulds
Everest World Match-Play:	Steve Davis
Norwich Union Grand Prix:	Steve Davis
Anglian British Open:	Tony Meo
Fersina Windows World Cup:	England (represented by Steve Davis, Neal Foulds and Jimmy White)
Matchroom League:	Steve Davis
Embassy World Championship:	Steve Davis

Top **They were all younger then! Steve, Barry, Doug Mountjoy, Geoff Foulds, referee John Smyth, Patsy Fagan, Dennis and Ray Reardon.** *Above* **Barry gives a winning salute, but did Steve and Tony really get on those horses?**

MATCHROOM

Chinese Chop Cuey

The first two ranking tournaments outside Britain were staged in 1988-89 in Canada and France. But who knows what the future holds? China could well stage a ranking tournament one day.

Barry Hearn has seen the Far East as a favourite growth area for a long time. During the last five years he has played more than a leading role – practically the only role in arousing and developing interest in such places as Hong Kong, Malaysia, Thailand, Japan, and, of course, China.

The Matchroom team first ventured into the Far East in 1982, when Steve and Tony made a triumphant visit to Thailand. Their matches against two local amateurs attracted 10 million viewers to live television coverage ... not bad considering the population of Thailand is only 46 million! Barry insisted on home players competing to arouse local interest. The welcome Steve and Tony got when they arrived at Bangkok airport was reminiscent of the Beatles arriving home from their US Tour in the 1960s.

Top **Dennis, Rex Williams, Tony, Willie, Neal and Barry Hearn in China with three members of the Chinese navy.** *Above* **Steve gets down to a trick shot in the Far East. Tony is the one who must not move a muscle.**

QUOTES...
FROM MATCHROOM PLAYERS

"Snooker will be like a locust swarm spreading across Asia" ... Barry Hearn

As he left Hong Kong station for Canton, Steve said: *"I'm off to preach the gospel of snooker"*

Noticing how many bicycles there were in China, Barry was quick to comment: *"How come they've never won the Tour de France?"*

A TOUCH OF EASTERN MAGIC

That was the start of the regular jaunt to the Far East which saw the return to Thailand in 1983 and the inauguration of the Camus Hong Kong Masters, which the then three Matchroom men (Steve, Tony and Terry) plus Doug Mountjoy contested. Mountjoy beat Terry 4-3 in the final (there's gratitude for Matchroom pioneering!) but Terry's 140 break, the highest ever in Hong Kong, excited the fans tremendously.

Since then the team has regularly made the trip to Hong Kong and Thailand and also taken in Singapore and Malaysia. Dubai, Japan and Brazil have also been ports of call for the globe-trotting cuemen as they have helped spread the gospel even wider. But the most exciting move in advancing snooker came in 1985 when Steve Davis and Dennis Taylor moved on from their traditional Far East trip and ventured into China, thanks to additional sponsorship from the cognac producers Camus.

Terry, Steve and Dennis repeated the trip in 1986 but the real breakthrough came in 1987 when Barry organised a £100,000 tournament in Peking, sponsored by British American Tobacco.

"TELLY'S ON THE TERRY"

The seven Matchroom men (Cliff wasn't with the team then) plus Rex Williams, along with eight local amateurs, made up a 16-strong field for the inaugural Kent Cup. And what a success it turned out to be! Television figures exceeded *100 million* for the final between Willie Thorne and Jimmy White. And the planned five hours coverage of the tournament was increased to ten and a half because of the interest.

Barry and the Matchroom boys have certainly played a significant role in helping snooker's advancement in the Far East. Where will it be next? Russia? The North Pole? Who knows . . . except Barry, that is!

From the top **Steve and Terry with friends in Dubai – the Matchroom boys are obviously lacking in headgear; Tony, Barry and Steve enjoy the exotic dancing in Thailand; the party and hosts for the Camus Masters in China – the** snooker men are *(back)* **John Parrott, Barry, Doug Mountjoy, Terry and Len Ganley, the referee;** *(front)* **Tony, Steve and Jimmy.**

THE MAGNIFICENT EIGHT

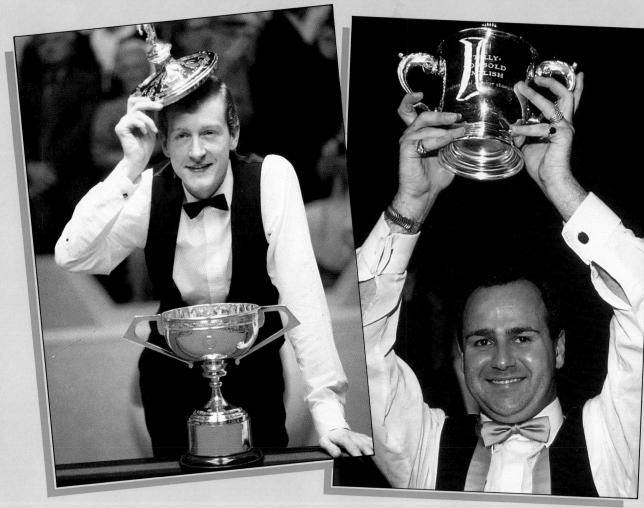

QUOTE FROM BARRY

When asked by Terry Wogan about snooker's power struggle Barry replied: *"Power struggle? What power struggle? It's been and gone, we won it . . ."* Read on and you will realise he was right!

We shouldn't need to tell you how good our magnificent eight are. You will no doubt have seen them often enough to form your own opinion. But let's have a look at their records which will leave you in no doubt as to their ability.

Since Matchroom was formed in the summer of 1982 there have been 39 ranking tournaments and 24 have been won by one of the team.

STEVE 19 THE REST 20

Steve obviously takes pride of place with 19 wins in that period. In other words, almost half of all ranking tournaments in seven years have been won by one player. That is quite a record in itself.

The other five Matchroom successes have been shared between three players: Jimmy with three wins, and Neal and Tony with one each. The other four members of the squad, while all winners in the past, have still, surprisingly, to win their first ranking tournament as a Matchroom player. The problem is, of course, with Steve winning so much – how can the others get a look in?

Left **Steve doffs his 'cap' after another of his wins (19 ranking tournaments) and** *(above)* **Tony after his Tolly Ales victory in 1987.**

DOUG FOILS CLEAN SWEEP

We started off last season by winning the first three ranking tournaments and were looking to equal our 1986-87 record, when we won all six tournaments. But that man Doug Mountjoy had other ideas and brought an end to our winning run. John Parrott thwarted a fourth triumph at Deauville when he beat Terry 9-8 in the final of the ICI European Open. But it was back to

RESULTS OF RANKING TOURNAMENT FINALS SINCE THE FORMATION OF MATCHROOM IN 1982

EMBASSY WORLD PROFESSIONAL CHAMPIONSHIP

1983	**Steve Davis** (Eng)	18-6	*Cliff Thorburn* (Can)	
1984	**Steve Davis** (Eng)	18-16	*Jimmy White* (Eng)	
1985	Dennis Taylor (Ire)	18-17	**Steve Davis** (Eng)	
1986	Joe Johnson (Eng)	18-12	**Steve Davis** (Eng)	
1987	**Steve Davis** (Eng)	18-14	Joe Johnson (Eng)	
1988	**Steve Davis** (Eng)	18-11	**Terry Griffiths** (Wal)	
1989	**Steve Davis** (Eng)	18-3	John Parrott (Eng)	

FIDELITY UNIT TRUSTS INTERNATIONAL

(Formerly Jameson International, Goya International, BCE International)

1982	Tony Knowles (Eng)	9-6	David Taylor (Eng)	
1983	**Steve Davis** (Eng)	9-4	*Cliff Thorburn* (Can)	
1984	**Steve Davis** (Eng)	9-2	Tony Knowles (Eng)	
1985	*Cliff Thorburn* (Can)	12-10	*Jimmy White* (Eng)	
1986	**Neal Foulds** (Eng)	12-9	*Cliff Thorburn* (Can)	
1987	**Steve Davis** (Eng)	12-5	*Cliff Thorburn* (Can)	
1988	**Steve Davis** (Eng)	12-6	**Jimmy White** (Eng)	

ROTHMANS GRAND PRIX

(formerly Professional Players Tournament)

1982	Ray Reardon (Wal)	10-5	*Jimmy White* (Eng)	
1983	Tony Knowles (Eng)	9-8	Joe Johnson (Eng)	
1984	*Dennis Taylor* (Ire)	10-2	*Cliff Thorburn* (Can)	
1985	**Steve Davis** (Eng)	10-9	**Dennis Taylor** (Ire)	
1986	**Jimmy White** (Eng)	10-6	Rex Williams (Eng)	
1987	Stephen Hendry (Sco)	10-7	**Dennis Taylor** (Ire)	
1988	**Steve Davis** (Eng)	10-6	Alex Higgins (Ire)	

BCE CANADIAN MASTERS

1988	**Jimmy White** (Eng)	9-4	**Steve Davis** (Eng)	

TENNENTS UK OPEN

(formerly Coral UK Open)

1984	**Steve Davis** (Eng)	16-8	Alex Higgins (Ire)	
1985	**Steve Davis** (Eng)	16-14	*Willie Thorne* (Eng)	
1986	**Steve Davis** (Eng)	16-7	**Neal Foulds** (Eng)	
1987	**Steve Davis** (Eng)	16-14	**Jimmy White** (Eng)	
1988	Doug Mountjoy (Wal)	16-12	Stephen Hendry (Sco)	

MERCANTILE CREDIT CLASSIC

(formerly Wilsons Classic, Lada Classic)

1984	**Steve Davis** (Eng)	9-8	**Tony Meo** (Eng)	
1985	*Willie Thorne* (Eng)	13-8	*Cliff Thorburn* (Can)	
1986	*Jimmy White* (Eng)	13-12	*Cliff Thorburn* (Can)	
1987	**Steve Davis** (Eng)	13-12	**Jimmy White** (Eng)	
1988	**Steve Davis** (Eng)	13-11 .	John Parrott (Eng)	
1989	Doug Mountjoy (Wal)	11-9	Wayne Jones (Wal)	

ICI EUROPEAN OPEN

1989	John Parrott (Eng)	9-8	**Terry Griffiths** (Wal)	

ANGLIAN BRITISH OPEN

(formerly Dulux British Open; MIM Britannia British Open)

1985	Silvino Francisco (SA)	12-9	Kirk Stevens (Can)	
1986	**Steve Davis** (Eng)	12-7	**Willie Thorne** (Eng)	
1987	**Jimmy White** (Eng)	13-9	**Neal Foulds** (Eng)	
1988	Stephen Hendry (Sco)	13-2	Mike Hallett (Eng)	
1989	**Tony Meo** (Eng)	13-6	Dean Reynolds (Eng)	

1. Players in **bold** were members of Matchroom at time of final
2. Players in *italic* were not Matchroom players at the time, but are current members of the team

RANKINGS 1989

1	(1)	**Steve Davis**
2	(7)	John Parrott
3	(4)	Stephen Hendry
4	(2)	**Jimmy White**
5	(5)	**Terry Griffiths**
6	(9)	Mike Hallett
7	(6)	**Cliff Thorburn**
8	(10)	**Dennis Taylor**
9	(13)	**Willie Thorne**
10	(24)	Doug Mountjoy
11	(11)	Joe Johnson
12	(8)	Tony Knowles
13	(15)	John Virgo
14	(31)	**Tony Meo**
15	(22)	Dean Reynolds
16	(32)	Steve James
19	(3)	**Neal Foulds**

MONEY WINNERS 1988-89

1	**Steve Davis**	£661,490
2	John Parrott	£314,394
3	Stephen Hendry	£310,171
4	**Jimmy White**	£263,859
5	Doug Mountjoy	£181,934
6	**Terry Griffiths**	£165,167
7	**Tony Meo**	£158,458
8	**Neal Foulds**	£142,343
9	**Dennis Taylor**	£132,041
10	Mike Hallett	£128,963
11	**Cliff Thorburn**	£126,275
12	**Willie Thorne**	£101,502
13	Alex Higgins	£100,664

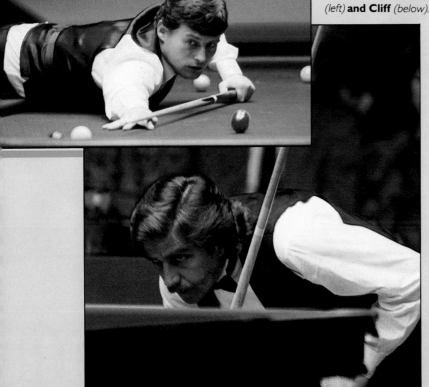

Numbers Seven and Eight of the Magnificent Eight, Jimmy *(left)* **and Cliff** *(below)*.

winning ways as Tony was the surprise winner of the Anglian Open and Steve won the Embassy for the third consecutive year to give Matchroom five of the eight ranking titles in 1988-89.

But our success is not only measured in terms of wins. Our strength in depth is our secret. You can be guaranteed at least one, and normally two, Matchroom players will make it to the last four of any major tournament. For that reason our players are constantly among the top money winners and the highest placed players in the rankings.

Just look at the results and tables. You won't need any more proof when we tell you the Matchroom boys are the most successful team ever in the world of professional snooker.

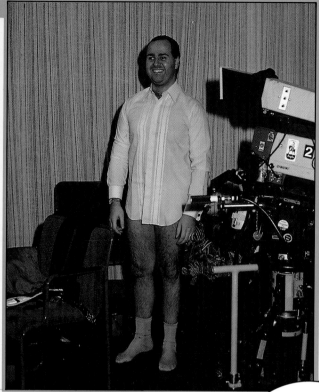

On the eve of the 1988 Tennents UK Championship the WPBSA announced fines totalling £34,000 on the Matchroom team for failing to give press interviews during the Rothmans Grand Prix. Steve had the biggest single fine imposed: £12,000.

Cliff Thorburn's 5-3 win over John Virgo in the fifth round of the Mercantile guaranteed him a cheque for £8,250. More significantly, it took the Matchroom team's cumulative winnings for the season beyond the £1 million mark for the third consecutive season, and six weeks quicker than it took to reach the milestone the previous season.

The last all-Welsh final in a major event before the 1989 Mercantile clash between Mountjoy and Jones, was in the 1980 Benson and Hedges Irish Masters, when Terry Griffiths beat Doug Mountjoy 9

The Terry Griffiths-Silvino Francisco match in the 1989 Benson and Hedges Masters attracted a crowd of just 294, the smallest ever for a snooker match at Wembley.

Joe Johnson was certainly in a hurry when he beat the "Hurricane", Alex Higgins 5-0 in the fourth round of the Mercantile . . . he was also in a hurry on his way to the event. The car he was in was stopped for speeding by the police!

The final of the 1989 Anglian British Open between Tony Meo and Dean Reynolds was the first ranking final to be contested by two left-handers.

Who said the French weren't ready for Snooker? . . . While walking around the Deauville Casino in his evening suit during the 1989 European Open, Irishman Eugene Hughes was asked for a drink. He was mistaken for one of the waiters.

The Silvino Francisco versus Paul Medati battle in the 1988 Tennents was a dour affair which the South African won 9-8 after eight hours play.

BEHIND THE

From the left: **Aren't you missing something, Tony? We all thought you were a natty dresser; Dennis and Cliff ready for a trip into the bush – where's the nearest billabong, boys?; No, it's not a wig, it's a handsome young Willie; Sadly Bill Werbeniuk said goodbye to professional snooker in 1989 when the WPSBA banned the drug he uses to keep his arm steady; Les Dodd, who twice threw away big leads in the Tennents.**

During the final of his Norwich Union European Grand Prix qualifier against Terry Griffiths in Milan, play was interrupted so the BBC could announce to Steve that he had won their Sports Personality of the Year Award for 1988.

The 1988 New Zealand Masters, won by Stephen Hendry, was played at the unlikely setting of the Government's Legislative Council Chambers in Wellington.

ny White beat WPBSA
rman John Virgo 5-2 in the
ning round of the 1989
son and Hedges Masters at
mbley. Virgo won the first two
mes, both on re-spotted blacks
rare occurrence.

Spare a thought for the ex-taxi driver Les Dodd. In the 1987 Tennents he led Dennis Taylor 8-2 and lost 9-8. A year later he led Alex Higgins 7-4 and lost 9-7.

The Cliff Thorburn-Eddie Charlton first-round match at The Crucible in 1989 took 10hr 24min to complete and ended at 2.39am. It is not the longest match, or latest finish, at The Crucible. It is, however, the longest first-round match.

The ninth game of the Rex Williams versus Bob Harris match in the 1988 Tennents had a 37-28 scoreline. It is believed to be the lowest scoring match in a ranking tournament.

'hen he compiled a 147
aximum against Jimmy White in
e 1989 Matchroom League at
awley, Cliff Thorburn became
e first man to compile two
icial maximum breaks.

Did you know that current professional Graham Cripsey spent 14 years as a Wall of Death rider in the family's business in Skegness before becoming a snooker professional?

Once, when in Hong Kong, Steve did a television advert for Camus brandy but with his voice dubbed in Chinese. We couldn't tell if the Chinese voice was slurred!

SCENES GOSSIP